D1460142

"At a time when some sections of the I elected to actively support and defend e violent religious forces in the name of anti ... 'anti-racism', the powerful arguments of this report are important – to generate debate and discussion, provoke challenges, and articulate the persistent opposition of the anti-war and socialist-feminist left to violations of human rights by Western powers, states and movements."

Chetan Bhatt,
London School of Economics and Political Science

"Meredith Tax cuts through right wing cant and left wing guilt, offering a subtle analysis of the double binds that weaken progressive political work. How can we protect the victim of US repression or brutality while at the same time criticizing and opposing that victim when he advocates for repressive theocratic states? Tax names a secular space where activists from both the Global South and North can meet as partners seeking democratic rule of law, religious pluralism, sexual freedom, and feminist understandings of women's rights. A tour de force."

Ann Snitow,
Director of Gender Studies at the New School University and founding member of the Network of East-West Women

"This is a brave and urgently necessary book – an invigorating counterblast against the pernicious notion that my enemy's enemy must be my friend even if that 'friend' wants to destroy all that we hold dear."

Francis Wheen,
author of *How Mumbo-Jumbo Conquered the World*

"This courageous book addresses the most difficult questions confronting emancipatory activists and movements today. It dispels some of the myths that paralyze and prevent them from criticizing and struggling against those who believe in and support blatant violations of human and women's rights. These myths include the ideas that the Muslim right is anti-imperialist, that 'defensive jihad' is the equivalent of national liberation struggles and that any critique of Islamism equals anti-Muslim racism."

Nira Yuval-Davis,
Director, Research Centre on Migration, Refugees and Belonging, UEL; a founder of Women Against Fundamentalism

DOUBLE BIND

The Muslim Right, the Anglo-American Left, and Universal Human Rights

Meredith Tax

Editorial Group: Ariane Brunet, Anissa Hélie, Sara Hossain and Gita Sahgal

CENTRE FOR SECULAR SPACE

ISBN : 978-0-9888303-0-1

www.centreforsecularspace.org
admin@centreforsecularspace.org

809 W. 181st Street, #210
New York, NY 10033

We gratefully acknowledge the support of the late Rhonda Copelon, the Feminist Press at CUNY, and the Jacob Blaustein Institute for the Advancement of Human Rights. This publication would not have been possible without their help and encouragement.

Book and cover design by Benjamin Mege

In memory of Rhonda Copelon,
a feminist lawyer who swam against the tide of the human rights
community to find ways to support victims of terrorism

CONTENTS

INTRODUCTION

In a period of right wing attacks on Muslims – or people thought to be Muslims – how does one respond to human rights violations by the Muslim Right without feeding hate campaigns?

When US diplomats invoke the oppression of Muslim women to sanctify war, how do we practice feminist solidarity without strengthening Orientalism and neocolonialism?

When the US targets jihadis for assassination by drone, should human rights defenders worry about violations perpetrated by those same jihadis or focus on violations by the state?

These are some of the questions raised in this study, which is a response to the way human rights organizations, the left and academic feminists think about terrorism and the Muslim Right. Even the use of the term "terrorism" invites criticism from the left, since it is often used by the state to repress anyone perceived as troublesome. We use the definition of the Office of the UN High Commissioner for Human Rights: "*Terrorism* is commonly understood to refer to acts of violence that target civilians in the pursuit of political or ideological aims ... Terrorism aims at the very destruction of human rights, democracy and the rule of law."[1]

Considering this definition, it is important to note that human rights violations by terrorists have drawn very little attention from human rights organizations or progressives, compared to violations by state counter-terrorism programmes. One reason is the traditional focus of human rights organizations upon the state.

---

[1] Office of the United Nations High Commissioner for Human Rights. Not dated. "Human Rights, Terrorism and Counter-terrorism". Fact Sheet No. 32.

But a deeper reason is that this terrain is tied up in knots by what Gregory Bateson called "the double bind," in which people are given conflicting instructions so that in obeying one set of orders, they must violate the other.

Human rights defenders must protect the rights of those oppressed by the state or by non-state actors. They must also defend the rights of women (which may be violated by the state as well as by non-state actors). But what happens when people mistreated by the state violate the rights of women? Can one fight their violations while at the same defending their rights against state power? How?

In the history of revolutions and the social movements of oppressed peoples, similar double binds have come up again and again. Frequently the response from the left and within social and national liberation movements has been to say that problems of women and gender will be dealt with later, after oppression by the state has been resolved. In the human rights world, on the other hand, the tendency has been to address women's and gender rights but in a way that compartmentalizes them, rather than recognizing that equality and non-discrimination are basic principles that should govern all work within the human rights framework.

The debate around Mona Eltahawy's May 2012 article on the oppression of women in the Middle East, called "Why do they hate us?"[2] is a recent example of the double bind. As Parastou Houssori, who teaches international refugee law at the University of Cairo, observed:

> Some of the other criticisms of El Tahawy's piece illustrate the dilemma of the "double bind" that African-American and other feminists have also faced.

---

[2] Eltawahy, M. 2012. "Why Do They Hate Us", *Foreign Policy*, 4 April.

For instance, when they write about their experiences, African-American feminists often find themselves caught between confronting the patriarchy within African-American communities, and defending their African-American brothers from the broader racism that exists in American society. Similarly, women who identify as Islamic feminists often find themselves in this bind, as they try to reconcile their feminism and religious identity, and also defend their religion from Islamophobia.[3]

Such double binds cannot be resolved by retreating into silence or becoming immobilized. As Bateson and others have discussed, this way schizophrenia lies. In international law, they must be addressed by widening the framework to include non-state actors, and by integrating equality and non-discrimination into human rights work. On the political level, one can only resolve them by thinking one's way through a maze of taboos, injunctions and received ideas as well as being willing to face backlash and censorship. Such is the task we have set ourselves in the following analysis.

Work on this publication began in 2010 when Gita Sahgal, former head of Amnesty International's gender unit, went public with her concerns about the organization's partnership with Cageprisoners, a group that advocates for prisoners of the "war on terror". She was suspended and a global controversy ensued that resulted in Amnesty International's endorsement of the doctrine of "defensive jihad".[4]

---

[3] Houssouri, P. 2012. "On 'Why Do They Hate Us?' and its Critics", *The Arabist*, 29 April.
[4] This phrase was used by Claudio Cordone, Interim Secretary General of Amnesty International from January to June 2010, in open letters to Amrita Chhachhi, Sara Hossain and Sunila Abeysekera, 28 February 2010 and 9 April 2012; see Tax, M. 2012. "Gitagate, Two Years After", *Dissent*, 27 June. www.dissentmagazine.org/blog/gitagate-two-years-after.

The next year, a group of feminist activists and writers who had come together around Sahgal's defence founded the Centre for Secular Space, a transnational think tank to strengthen secular voices, oppose fundamentalism and promote universality in human rights. As one of their first projects, they decided to finish and expand an analysis of Cageprisoners begun the previous year by Sukhwant Dhaliwal and Pragna Patel, members of Women Against Fundamentalism and Southall Black Sisters. The result is this publication, which was written by Meredith Tax with an editorial group consisting of Ariane Brunet, Anissa Hélie, Sara Hossain, and Gita Sahgal.

While the programme of the Centre for Secular Space addresses problems raised by many kinds of religious fundamentalism, we feel a responsibility to sum up an historic debate within the human rights movement of which we are a part. For this reason, our first two publications are this book and a forthcoming documentary history of the controversy over Amnesty International and Cageprisoners.

As longtime activists in many progressive movements, we believe that any political transformation worthy of the name must be based on universal human rights, and that secular space is an essential – though not a sufficient – condition for the exercise of these rights. We are thus concerned when human rights organizations, the left and feminists ally themselves politically with the Muslim Right, just as we are when they ally with the Christian, Jewish, Hindu, Buddhist, Sikh or nationalist Right.

It is difficult to address issues involving the Muslim Right in the current climate of increasing xenophobia, discrimination and violent attacks upon Muslims in both Europe and North America. We know that Islam is often maligned and misrepresented in the North. We agree that jihadis have the same rights to due process of law as anybody else, and should be defended against violations like rendition and torture. But that should not mean giving their ideas political support, as happens when human rights organizations endorse "defensive jihad" or antiwar coalitions allow sex-segregated seating at their meetings.

This study is organized as follows:

Section I goes over some recent history and defines terms. What is the Muslim Right? What are the differences between what the press calls "moderate Islamists" and jihadis? Why is Afghanistan central to the modern narrative of jihad? What do salafi-jihadis believe and how do they organize?

Section II is about terrorism, what it means and why it must be addressed in terms of human rights. It discusses Guantanamo and touches on distortions in the practice of human rights organizations in relation to jihadi victims of the "war on terror".

Section III is a case study of Cageprisoners, which bills itself as a human rights organization defending prisoners at Guantanamo and other prisoners of the "war on terror". Cageprisoners has partnered with human rights groups like Amnesty International, Reprieve and the Center for Constitutional Rights, and it is funded by the Rowntree Trust. We demonstrate that it is actually a public relations organization for salafi-jihadi propaganda groups and individuals that uses human rights language as political cover for an ideology completely opposed to universal human rights.

Section IV turns from the human rights movement to the Anglo-American left; it discusses left wing support for the Muslim Right and gives a brief account of this support within the antiwar movement.

Section V addresses five wrong ideas about the Muslim Right: that it is anti-imperialist; that "defence of Muslim lands" is comparable to national liberation struggles; that the problem is "Islamophobia"; that terrorism is justified by revolutionary necessity; and that any feminist who criticizes the Muslim Right is an Orientalist and ally of US imperialism.

Section VI argues that the left and feminists should show solidarity not with the Muslim Right but with leftists, feminists and secularists who are fighting fundamentalism in the Global South and in ethnic and minority communities of the North.

THE MUSLIM RIGHT

"MODERATE ISLAMISTS", SALAFIS AND SALAFI-JIHADIS

The Muslim Right is a range of transnational political movements that mobilize identity politics towards the goal of a theocratic state. It consists of those the media call "moderate Islamists", who aim to reach this goal gradually by electoral and educational means;[5] extremist parties and groups called "salafis" that may run for office but also try to enforce some version of Sharia law through street violence; and a much smaller militant wing of salafi-jihadis[6] that endorses military means and practices violence against civilians. The goal of all political Islamists, whatever means they may prefer, is a state founded upon a version of Sharia law that systematically discriminates against women along with sexual and religious minorities.

---

[5] Moderate Islamist groups work through elections, education, propaganda, charity and organizing. They include Turkey's Justice and Development Party (AKP), Tunisia's Ennahda, and the transnational networks Hizb ut-Tahrir, the Muslim Brotherhood and Jamaat-e-Islami, which have many local front organizations. In some countries, like Algeria, Egypt, Kuwait, Lebanon and Yemen, salafis have also formed political parties and run for election without being in the least "moderate" or relinquishing violence.

The story of "moderate Islamists" and salafi political groups, and their sometimes fraught, sometimes friendly relations with states in North Africa, the Middle East, and South Asia, as well as in the US and Western Europe, is a long and complex one that falls outside the scope of this analysis. The following story concerns salafi-jihadis, and, like so many political stories, it begins with the Cold War.

THE FIRST AFGHAN WAR AND THE BIRTH OF AL-QAEDA

The Cold War pitted the US and Western democracies against the socialist countries, particularly the Soviet bloc, for the allegiance of the peoples of the Global South. In 1978, Marxist revolutionaries allied to the Soviet Union overthrew the Afghan government; they instituted land reform, declared equality for women and repressed the opposition. The US began secretly recruiting warlords and Islamist mujahideen to

---

[6] The term "salafi-jihadis" was coined by French researcher Gilles Kepel to describe very strict Islamists (salafis) involved in violent jihad, particularly those in al-Qaeda. According to Kepel, salafism-jihadism combines "respect for the sacred texts in their most literal form ... with an absolute commitment to jihad, whose number one target had to be America, perceived as the greatest enemy of the faith." Livesey, B. 2005. "The Salafist Movement", *Frontline*, 25 January. Salafi-jihadi groups include: al-Qaeda and its various branches; the groups of the "Iraqi insurgency"; Lashkar-e-Taiba in Kashmir; the Taliban in Afghanistan and Pakistan; the Algerian Armed Islamic Group (GIA) and Islamic Salvation Front (FIS) in Algeria; Ansar Dine and MUJAO in Mali; Boko Haram in Nigeria; al-Shabaab in Somalia; the Sudanese National Islamic Front (which seized power in 1989); and Jemaah Islamiyah in Indonesia. There are also salafi-jihadi groups in Azerbaijan, Chechnya and most of the "stans" of Central Asia, as well as the Moro Islamic Liberation Front and other armed groups in the Philippines.

fight the new government, hoping that the Soviet Union would intervene and exhaust itself in a Russian version of Vietnam.[7]

The Soviets invaded in 1979. At that point, a radical Islamist scholar named Abdullah Azzam – a key figure in the Muslim Brotherhood, who was originally from Palestine but had taught in Saudi Arabia and was now teaching in Pakistan – issued a fatwa, *Defence of the Muslim Lands: The First Obligation after Imam*.[8]

Azzam said that defence of Muslim lands against invaders was an obligation and called upon young men to come to Afghanistan and fight the Soviets. With money and help from Osama bin Laden, a rich Saudi who came to work with him, Azzam set up the Afghan Services Bureau, which bought air tickets for foreign fighters to come to Peshawar, established guest houses for them, organized military training camps, and recruited thousands of foreign mujahideen, soon called the "Arab-Afghans". The US, Saudi Arabia and Pakistan all helped finance and equip the "Arab-Afghans" because they wanted them to fight communism. The US and Saudi Arabia channeled most of their aid through Pakistan's Inter-services Intelligence (ISI).[9]

Ten years of war ensued. By 1989, the Soviet Union was in the process of dissolution and pulled its troops out of Afghanistan. Once the Soviets were gone, the US lost interest in the region. A communist government held on until 1992, when a coalition government succeeded it. At that point Gulbuddin Hekmatyar,

---

[7] Cockburn, A. and J. St. Clair. 1998. "Zbigniew Brzezinski: How Jimmy Carter and I Started the Mujahideen", *Counterpunch*, 15 January.
[8] Azzam, A. Not dated. *Defence of the Muslim Lands: The First Obligation after Imam*. *Religioscope*. www.religioscope.com/info/doc/jihad/azzam_defence_1_table.htm.
[9] Hiro, D. 1999. "The Cost of an Afghan 'victory'", *The Nation*, 15 February.

a warlord supported by Pakistan, began bombing Kabul. Hostilities broke out between Hekmatyar and competing groups of warlords supported by Iran and Saudi Arabia, and the country plunged into civil war once more.

While all this was happening in northern Afghanistan, an armed group called the Taliban, founded in Pakistan, consolidated its power in Kandahar in the south. The Taliban instituted an extreme form of Islamist rule in which women were forbidden to work outside the home, go to school, or leave the house without being accompanied by a male relative – even if they had no living male relatives or had to go to the hospital. Kite flying, music and mixed gatherings were also forbidden, and men were forced to grow beards. All these were violations of the most basic human rights including the right to freedom of movement, the right to freedom from arbitrary interference, the right to education, the right to work and the right to equality before the law.

In 1996, Ahmad Shah Massoud, defence minister of the coalition government in Kabul, attempted to form a national alliance. The Taliban refused to join, and with military support from Pakistan and economic support from Saudi Arabia, moved north, captured Kabul and proclaimed the Emirate of Afghanistan. Massoud then formed the Northern Alliance to fight the Taliban, and the civil war continued. Only three countries recognized the Taliban government: Pakistan, Saudi Arabia, and the United Arab Emirates.

The Taliban committed a number of massacres during the civil war, notably against Shi'a Muslims and the Hazara ethnic minority. Some eight thousand Shi'a were murdered in 1998 when the Taliban captured Mazar-el-Sharif. At the time, the Taliban commander declared, "Hazaras are not Muslim, they are Shi'a. They are *kufr* [infidels, also spelled *kuffar*]."[10]

Osama bin Laden led a brigade of Arab fighters aiding the Taliban; they were responsible for many civilian deaths and in 2001 succeeded in assassinating Ahmad Shah Massoud. But bin Laden was also looking farther afield; as early as 11 February 1988, he and Abdullah Azzam had held a secret meeting with leaders of Egyptian Islamic Jihad at which they agreed to internationalize the struggle after the Soviets were defeated.[11] This was the founding meeting of al-Qaeda.

During the period of civil war and Taliban rule, young men from many countries, including Moazzam Begg from the UK and later of Cageprisoners, found their way to Afghanistan. The Taliban re-opened the training camps that had been set up by the US Central Intelligence Agency (CIA) and ISI during the war against the Soviets and began "to give guerrilla training to fundamentalist volunteers from Xinjiang, China; Bosnia; Algeria; and elsewhere to further their Islamist agenda through armed actions in their respective countries."[12] Some of these mujahideen went on to fight in civil wars in various Muslim countries; others joined al-Qaeda.

Young men went to fight in Afghanistan for many reasons; religious fervour, anger at Serbian atrocities during the Bosnian war, unemployment, lack of a future in their own countries, disenfranchisement, racism, dictatorship. Not everyone who trained in Afghanistan became an active fighter; some supported the struggle in other ways. But most of those who went to Afghanistan to support the Taliban were sympathetic to its politics and serious enough to act upon those sympathies. In fact, Taliban supporters like Moazzam Begg saw Afghanistan as exemplifying a return to original Muslim values. According to

---

[10] Hiro, op. cit.
[11] Wright, L. 2006. *The Looming Tower*. New York: Knopf, p. 133.
[12] Hiro, op. cit.

Chetan Bhatt, Director of the Centre for the Study of Human Rights at the London School of Economics, Afghanistan was the central, indispensable location in the struggle for Islamic purity.

> For global visionaries who inhabited a specific political-intellectual universe, Taliban Afghanistan had a world-historic significance. It was apprehended as a near-perfect state and society by Barot[13] and Omar Khyam, a central figure in the 2004 "fertilizer bomb" plot. It was also viewed as an ideal base for military training that had to be protected from Western interference.[14]

Illustrating Bhatt's point, Pakistani nuclear scientist Sultan Bashiruddin Mahmood described Afghanistan as the "ideal Islamic state", and set up an organization, UTN (Ummah Tameer-e-Nau), to help the Taliban.[15] (This was later declared a terrorist organization after a search of its office in Kabul unearthed plans to kidnap a US diplomat and learn how to build nuclear weapons.) Sufi Muhammad bin Alhazrat Hassan, founder of Tehreek-e-Nafaz-e-Shariat-e-Mohammadi (TNSM) – banned in Pakistan in 2002 as a terrorist organization after it tried to impose Sharia law in the province of Swat[16] – told a reporter that he hated democracy, wanted to impose Islamic rule throughout the world, and believed that the Taliban was "an ideal example" of what needed to be done in Pakistan.[17] To Moazzam Begg, the Taliban was "upholding pure, old Islamic values".[18]

---

[13] Dhiren Barot, a UK-born al-Qaeda figure convicted of terrorism and currently imprisoned in the UK.
[14] Bhatt, C. 2009. "The 'British Jihad' and the Curve of Religious Violence", *Ethnic and Racial Studies*, Volume 33, Issue 1, 28 September.
[15] Rondeaux, C. 2008. "Former Pakistan Intelligence Official Denies Aiding Group Tied to Mumbai Seige", *Washington Post*, 9 December.
[16] Yusef, H. 2009. "Tacit Support for Violence?" *Dawn*, 4 September.

In fact, many of these values, now invoked by salafi-jihadis all over the world, were neither pure nor old, but modern imports from Saudi Arabia. The claim is political, not historical.

THE ROLE OF SAUDI ARABIA

The Saudis played a germinal role in the development of the salafi-jihadi movement throughout Asia. According to the late Richard Holbrooke, a US diplomat, Saudi-financed madrassahs (religious schools) are factories for salafi-jihadism from Bangladesh and Pakistan to the new states of Central Asia.[19] Pakistani physicist and social critic Pervez Hoodbhoy concurs: "All this hard line Islam is traceable to Saudi Arabia."[20] Professor Vali Nasr, Dean of the Johns Hopkins School of Advanced International Studies, amplifies:

> Saudi Arabia has been the single biggest source of funding for fanatical interpretations of Islam, and the embodiment of that interpretation in organizations and schools has created a self-perpetuating institutional basis for promoting fanaticism across the Muslim world. ... There is no other state [that] spends as much money [on] ensuring conservatism and fanaticism among Muslims.[21]

[17] Roggio, B. "Analysis: Pakistan Peace Agreement Cedes Ground to the Taliban". *Long War Journal*. 18 February 2009. www.longwarjournal. org/archives/2009/02/analysis_pakistan_pe.php.
[18] Begg, M. with V. Brittain. 2006. *Enemy Combatant: a British Muslim's Journey to Guantanamo and Back*. New York: The New Press, p. 381.
[19] "Interview with Richard Holbrooke", *Frontline*, October 2001. www.pbs.org/ wgbh/pages/frontline/shows/saudi/interviews/holbrooke.html.
[20] Walsh, D. 2011. "Saudi Arabian charity in Pakistan offers education – or is it extremism?" *The Guardian*, 29 June.
[21] "Interview Vali Nasr", *Frontline*, 25 October 2001. www.pbs.org/ wgbh/pages/frontline/shows/saudi/interviews/nasr.html.

The Independent published a report in 2007 on Saudi financing, which stated:

> Saudi Arabia's brand of Islam, the ultra-conservative Wahhabism, has been exported globally and is followed by al-Qaeda and other Sunni fundamentalist groups responsible for terrorist attacks around the world. Funding for such groups comes from charitable organizations and wealthy individuals in Saudi Arabia and other Gulf states ... In the decade up to 2002, according to a report to the UN Security Council, al-Qaeda and other Islamist bodies collected between £150m and £250m, mostly from Saudi charities and private donors. This practice is still occurring, with Saudi Arabia linked to funding Sunni jihadists in Iraq.[22]

Similarly, in cables released by Wikileaks in 2010, US Secretary of State Hillary Clinton acknowledges that Saudi donors are the most significant source of support for salafi-jihadi groups worldwide, including al-Qaeda, the Taliban and Pakistan's Lashkar-e-Taiba, and that despite the US-Saudi alliance, the US has not been able to put a dent in this support.

> While the Kingdom of Saudi Arabia (KSA) takes seriously the threat of terrorism within Saudi Arabia, it has been an ongoing challenge to persuade Saudi officials to treat terrorist financing emanating from Saudi Arabia as a strategic priority.[23]

---

[22] Cochrane, P. 2007. "Terror finance trail vanishes in Saudi Arabia", *The Independent*, 30 September.
[23] "Wikileaks: Saudis 'chief funders of Sunni militants'", *BBC News*, 5 December 2010.

Drawing on the work of French political scientist Giles Kepel, Leila Ahmed, a professor at the Harvard Divinity School, sums up the role of the US-Saudi alliance in the development of modern jihadism:

> Following the Soviet Union's invasion of Afghanistan in 1979, the United States and Saudi Arabia joined forces, out of their shared hatred for the Soviet Union and its "godless empire", to defeat communism in Afghanistan. Saudi Arabia encouraged its youth to go to Afghanistan to fight the jihad against the Soviet Union. In Washington, the Reagan Administration had elevated Wahhabism [the extremely conservative Saudi form of Islam] "to the status of liberation theology – one that would free the region of communism". The jihadists, dubbed "freedom fighters", were "trained and equipped by the CIA and supported by petro-dollars from the Arabian Peninsula". Fighters were recruited elsewhere in the Arab and Muslim world. When Egypt, in the mid-eighties, released Islamists jailed in connection with Sadat's assassination, they were sent on pilgrimage to Mecca, and from there they boarded flights to Pakistan to fight the communists in Afghanistan.[24]

Under the Reagan administration (1981-1989), the US became a prime fundraising and recruiting location for the Afghan jihad. The Afghan Services Bureau operated by Abdullah Azzam and Osama bin Laden opened recruiting bureaus in thirty-three US cities; Islamic student associations at universities also became recruiting grounds.[25] When the Soviet Union left Afghanistan in 1989, Azzam and bin Laden's recruits fought alongside the Taliban

---

[24] Ahmed, L. 2011. *A Quiet Revolution: The Veil's Resurgence from the Middle East to America.* New Haven: Yale University Press, p.177.
[25] *Ibid*, p. 178.

to take over the country. When the Taliban captured Kabul in 1992, the foreign recruits, or "Arab-Afghans", were free to take their skills and weapons to other parts of the world.

SALAFI-JIHADI IDEOLOGY

What do salafi-jihadis believe, and how do these beliefs relate to universal human rights? In 2006, AWAAZ-South Asia Watch, a group of London scholars and activists who originally came together to oppose the Hindu Right, produced a pioneering piece of research called, "The Islamic Right – Key Tendencies". It identifies the following themes as the markers of salafi-jihadi ideology:

■ A "return" to the *salaf*,[26] which they claim is the same as the actual early history of Islam as exemplified by the first generations of Muslims, their beliefs and practices; this typically entails rejecting some or all of the entire canon of Islamic historical-legal traditions.

■ A belief in the imposition of Sharia[27] upon all Muslims, and the added belief that they know what Sharia is, and that their particular version of Sharia is the only correct one.

---

[26] *Salaf* means ancestors, referring to those alive during the lifetime of the Prophet Mohammed; salafis wish to get rid of all the history and interpretations since that time.

[27] As described by Fred Halliday, "Sharia law is a generic term for divinely sanctioned Islamic law, now a talisman invoked by fundamentalists without historical or canonical authority." Halliday, F. 2010. *Shocked and Awed.* Berkeley: University of California Press, p. 170. In reality, as Women Living Under Muslim Laws explains, "There is no such thing as the one, uniform Islamic set of laws; there is no such thing as a codified Sharia. There are, however, four different schools of Islamic law, the art of arguing and interpreting various legal sources, and centuries-old debates. In this arena, culture, religion, and politics are merged by social and state forces with a view to controlling people, especially women." Nouria Ali-Tani. 2011. *"Profile of Women Living Under Muslim Laws: What's in a Name?"*, Goethe-Institut, *Fikrun Wa Fann*, Jan. www.goethe.de/ges/phi/prj/ffs/the/ger/en7088997.htm.

—   A deep sectarianism, especially among the salafi tendencies, which often manifests itself in claiming to be able to define who is the true Muslim and who is not.

—   A belief that only (their favoured) clerics can know, define and interpret the will and intention of God.

—   An aim to seriously curtail women's rights, freedoms and liberties, and place women primarily in a domestic and child-rearing role.

—   A deeply conservative or authoritarian view of the family, gender roles and issues of sexuality.

—   An inherently undemocratic worldview, moreover one in which other minority rights should be diminished or erased.

—   A belief in jihad such that jihad is *primarily* defined as physical fighting (*qital*), or the use of one's wealth for the purposes of supporting physical fighting, in the path of whatever is interpreted to be the way of God.

—   A chauvinism regarding other beliefs, religious or otherwise.

—   A view of faith and politics as inherently the same and to be mixed together, such that religion is something that has to be regularly politicized.

—   A belief in the ultimate goal of an Islamic state (and their interpretation of Sharia) as the answer to all of the problems affecting humanity in general and Muslims in particular.[28]

---

[28] AWAAZ-South Asia Watch. June 2006. "The Islamic Right – Key Tendencies". www.centreforsecularspace.org/?q=resources.

It should be noted that many points in the list could apply to Catholic, Protestant evangelical and Jewish fundamentalists. They also oppose equal rights for women, focus on rigid gender roles and tight control of sexuality, and, because they believe their code comes directly from God, are sectarian and undemocratic, though only some embrace violence or want to set up a global religious state.

To salafi-jihadis, it is basic that there should be no separation between religion and politics; it is an obligation to ensure that other Muslims accept their definition of the faith. Therefore the defence of "Muslim lands" applies not only to countries that have been invaded by the West, but also to Muslim-majority countries that practice alternate forms of Islam and thus must be brought to correct fundamentalist belief. Shi'ites, Sufis and Ahmadis are considered *kuffar* (unbelievers); Christians and Jews, while "people of the book", are also unbelievers; and Hindus and atheists are of an even lower order. Salafi-jihadis therefore have a rather long list of countries targeted as places to defend by fighting. In his fatwa, "Defence of Muslim Lands", Abdullah Azzam listed some of them:

> The sin upon this present generation, for not advancing towards Afghanistan, Palestine, the Philippines, Kashmir, Lebanon, Chad, Eritrea etc, is greater than the sin inherited from the loss of the lands [that] have previously fallen into the possession of the Kuffar. We have to concentrate our efforts on Afghanistan and Palestine now, because they have become our foremost problems.[29]

---

[29] Azzam, op cit.

A similar list of target countries, along with the themes identified by AWAAZ, can be found in the writings or testimony of virtually every salafi-jihadi convicted on terrorist charges since 2001 and many others, such as Anwar al-Awlaki, the US citizen who was a propagandist for al-Qaeda and one of its leaders in the Arabian Peninsula until he was assassinated by US drone in September 2011.

In 2005, Al-Awlaki recorded a series of extremely popular CD-ROM lectures called *Constants on the Path to Jihad*,[30] which were published by Maktabah al-Ansar, a radical Islamist bookstore in Birmingham.[31] This work consists of al-Awlaki's commentaries on a text by Yusuf al Uyayri, a leader of al-Qaeda in the Arabian Peninsula who was killed in 2003. Al Uyayri was the author of several key salafi-jihadi texts that validate suicide bombers and their actions in which civilians (Muslim or otherwise) could be killed. It is clear that al-Awlaki selected this work to promote in keeping with his own views. His basic message is that military jihad is obligatory regardless of circumstances. Here is a summary of the propositions he endorses in *Constants*, which are not tenets of most varieties of Islam but are central to salafi-jihadi belief:

— Jihad is physical fighting, or material support for physical fighting; this has been prescribed by God until the Day of Judgment "since we are told to wipe out *kufr* from the world".[32]

---

[30] Al-Uyayri, Y. Not dated. *Constants on the Path of Jihad [Thawaabit,ala darb al-Jihad]*. Lecture Series delivered by Anwar al-Awlaki, transcribed and edited by "Mujahid fe Sabeelillah". Available for download on many websites.
[31] This bookstore was founded by Moazzam Begg but he left it in 2001 to live in Afghanistan under the Taliban, and it was being run by someone else in 2005 when it published *Constants*.
[32] *Constants*, op. cit., p. 19.

— Jihad is obligatory on every capable Muslim.[33]

— Jihad is global. It is not a local phenomenon. The reason that jihad has to be global is that "our enemy is neither a nation or a race. It is a system of *kuffar* with global reach."[34]

— Offensive jihad (physical fighting to propagate Islam as opposed to fighting to defend Muslims under attack) is mandatory and should be undertaken by Muslims at least once a year.[35]

— There is no distinction between the killing of civilians and non-civilians.[36]

— Jihad is not the same as a national liberation struggle; the only thing to be considered is the interests of the religion of Allah, not of any nation. It has nothing to do with war or invasions or occupations; it is not restricted to any time or place but is an obligation for all time that continues until the end of time.[37]

— The intended outcome of jihad is to establish the *umma* [Muslim community] as a global caliphate in which disbelievers will be either "wiped out" or living under Sharia as religious minorities.[38]

---

[33] *Constants*, op. cit., p. 63.
[34] *Ibid.*, p. 32.
[35] *Ibid.*, p. 35.
[36] *Ibid.*, pp. 15-17, 52.
[37] *Ibid.*, pp. 31-39, 42.
[38] Al-Awlaki, A. Not dated. "How to Establish the Khilifah by Shaykh Anwar Al Awlaki". www.kalamullah.com/manhaj21.html.

For those who die in battle, al-Awlaki says: "When the *kuffar* see you die in the path of Allah, they think its victory when in reality, you have won. The *kuffar* have given you a free ticket to Paradise." Similarly, "Our culture of martyrdom needs to be revived because the enemy of Allah fears nothing more than our love for death."[39] This is a clear endorsement of suicide bombings.

SALAFI-JIHADI ORGANIZATION

There is considerable disagreement among experts regarding the organizational form of al-Qaeda and jihadi organizational structure in general. According to Chetan Bhatt, "Of key significance are ideological groups organized around (now former) key bookshops in the UK."[40]

In other words, one of the salient aspects of support for salafi-jihadi activism is propaganda, and the use of certain radical mosques and bookstores as gathering and distribution points. Maktabah al-Ansar, the bookstore and publishing house co-founded by Moazzam Begg in Birmingham in 1998, was such a centre of ideological support, as is his current organization, Cageprisoners, which we will address in more detail in Section III.

No movement involving armed struggle is made up exclusively of fighters; terrorist groups in particular need many forms of support. They need logistical support from people who can move money, establish safe houses, forge passports and visas, and purchase materials and weapons. They need ideological, political, and practical support from writers and propagandists

---

[39] *Constants*, op. cit., p. 53; *44 Ways*, op. cit., p. 2.
[40] Bhatt, op. cit., pp. 9-10.

who can explain the movement's goals in a way that makes them attractive. They must also promote heroic figures as examples, arrange speaking engagements and meetings, produce websites and videos, run bookstores, and penetrate the broader society to find sympathizers, donors, and potential recruits.

Counter-terrorism strategies make little distinction between active fighters and their ideological supporters, assuming that anyone who supports jihadis is a potential suicide bomber. Not only does the counter-terrorist apparatus violate human rights standards by using methods like kidnapping and torture, it also entraps people who might never have done anything without prompting from the Federal Bureau of Investigation. On the other hand, as will be discussed in Section IV, some prominent players in the human rights movement and the left have made the opposite error, assuming that everyone who is accused of being a terrorist is innocent. They thus sanitize violations of human rights and promote individuals who openly support such violations.

It is critical to distinguish between belief and action. Democracy depends on the right of free expression. Nobody should be killed, locked up, or put on trial merely for expressing his or her opinions, no matter how repellant those opinions may be; no crime is committed unless the words lead directly to violence against others. On the other hand, people should be held politically responsible for their opinions, particularly when those opinions support violence against others. Advocating salafi-jihadi ideas gives them political support.

A similar standard should be applied to Moazzam Begg and others who supported the Taliban. When it was in power, the Taliban violated human rights in multiple ways, for instance, confining women to their homes, stoning people accused of immorality, organizing pogroms against Muslims of different belief, blowing up the Bamayan buddhas, and making non-Muslims such as Sikhs wear yellow badges.[41] Those who supported them were endorsing a twenty-first century form of religious fascism. Nobody who supports any form of fascism should be seen as a human rights defender, whether or not he was imprisoned in Guantanamo. But the excesses of the "war on terror" have served to blur these distinctions.

---

[41] Yusufzai-Jang, R. 2001. "Taliban and Afghan Hindus", *The News, Afghanistan News Center*, 28 May. Singh, H. 2001. "Taliban and the colour yellow", *The Indian Express*, 29 May. Commentators noted that this was a clear imitation of Nazi policy towards Jews prior to the decision to exterminate them.

TERRORISM AND UNIVERSAL HUMAN RIGHTS

Since 9/11, the world has been caught in what human rights law professor Karima Bennoune calls the paradigm of "Terror/Torture".[42] The US kidnaps, tortures, and uses drones to assassinate those it considers to be terrorists, often killing civilians at the same time. Militant Islamists kidnap and assassinate both officials and civilians, and blow themselves up along with anyone nearby. And while national security experts analyze terrorist movements and human rights organizations defend those accused of terrorism, very few people – mainly feminists – have addressed terrorism in terms of the human rights of civilians. Over the years, this gap in the discussion has formed a dangerous vacuum.

Why is this a problem? Because terrorism and counter-terrorism cannot be separated, they are the two sides of a dialectic. Like conjoined twins, they are formed in relation to one another and locked in continual struggle, and both affect the enjoyment of human rights, including the right to life itself. Counter-terrorist violations of human rights include denial of due process of law, kidnapping, sexual assault, arbitrary detention, rendition, torture, targeted assassination, and repressive measures used to stifle the voices of human rights defenders.

---

[42] Bennoune, K. 2008. "Terror/Torture", *Berkeley Journal of International Law*, v. 26:1.

But terrorism involves similar grave human rights abuses, as the Office of the UN High Commissioner for Human Rights points out:

> Terrorism aims at the very destruction of human rights, democracy and the rule of law. It attacks the values that lie at the heart of the Charter of the United Nations and other international instruments: respect for human rights; the rule of law; rules governing armed conflict and the protection of civilians; tolerance among peoples and nations; and the peaceful resolution of conflict.[43]

This kind of analysis from the human rights community is comparatively rare. More common is a one-sided focus on counter-terrorism, rather than a balanced approach to violations by both state and non-state actors. Human rights discussions of terrorism and counter-terrorism also demonstrate a desire to avoid issues of political affiliation and belief. But these cannot be avoided. While left wing terrorists still exist in places like Colombia, India, Nepal and Peru, in today's world most terrorist movements are rooted in right wing identity politics, and mobilize religion and culture to gain political power.[44]

Just as counter-terrorist violations affect the human rights of some, violations by fundamentalist extremists threaten the

---

[43] Office of the United Nations High Commissioner for Human Rights, op. cit.
[44] Examples include the current campaign by US evangelical Christians to make homosexuality a capital crime in Uganda; the 2002 Gujarat anti-Muslim riots orchestrated by Hindu extremists with support from the Bharatiya Janata Party (BJP) state government; Islamist mob attacks on the film *Persepolis* just prior to the Tunisian election; and attacks on US abortion clinics including bombings, arson and the murder of clinic personnel.

liberty and security of others. Most fundamentalist campaigns are local; events like 7/7 in the UK and 9/11 in the US are rare compared to pressure, threats and violence at the community level, designed to impose ideological conformity and obedience to fundamentalist rules. The continuum begins with authoritarian control of communities by non-state actors using means that range from social and economic pressure to the threat and exercise of violence. The goal of these non-state actors may be disruption of the state with the ultimate aim of replacing it, or it may be control of their own religious or ethnic group, but in either case they exercise most of their pressure and violence not upon the state but on civilian communities they consider to be their base. One of their aims is to impose their moral values on such communities, which usually entails targeting religious minorities, women, and LGBT populations. In situations where fundamentalists control the state, their ability to terrorize local communities and persecute free thinkers, sexual and religious minorities and women is even greater.

Non-state actors spread terror among selected civilian populations using propaganda, group pressure and acts of violence to constitute themselves as the "moral leaders" of the community: gang-raping lesbians to "cure" them; lynching blacks who try to buy property on the white side of town; assaulting women who wear sleeveless blouses; beating or killing unmarried men and women seen together in the street.

Fundamentalists commit a range of human rights violations to terrorize communities into submission, including torture, rape, murder and the threat of violence; execution for adultery; execution of abortion providers; and a system of house arrest that forbids women leaving home without a male escort, thus preventing many from working, going to school, or getting medical care. They justify such human rights violations by saying they are ordered by God. Today many of the sharpest attacks on freedom of expression and thought, freedom of religious belief, reproductive rights, gender, and freedom of movement are waged by those who claim to be defenders of religious values and cultural traditions.

None of this is meant to excuse or sanitize counter-terrorist human rights violations by the US and its allies. The name Guantamano has become synonymous with a series of sustained and systematic violations of international law by the US and its allies, including the practice known as "extraordinary rendition", which means kidnapping people and flying them to secret detention centres around the world for interrogation under torture while denying them access to courts and lawyers. As Moazzam Begg has acknowledged, conditions at Guantanamo are not the worst among these secret detention sites; there is far less oversight of some other detention centres, such as Bagram in Afghanistan. But as the most visible detention facility, Guantanamo has become the symbol of some of the worst counter-terrorist violations of human rights, including the use of torture, which is prohibited in all circumstances under international standards. The continued use of the prison to keep some terrorist suspects in indefinite detention is an everlasting blot on the human rights record of the US.

It is critically important for defenders of human rights to continue to track state violations committed in the name of counter-terrorism. But it is also incumbent upon human rights organizations to scrutinize the ideology of groups they defend, and to make it clear that while they may defend the human rights of those accused of terrorism, they do not support their beliefs. That includes being vigilant against the tendency to cover up these beliefs by failing to mention them when defending fundamentalists whose own rights have been violated by the US. Because of the centrality of Guantanamo to US counter-terrorism policy, the story of Cageprisoners, a British organization headed by a former Guantanamo detainee, Moazzam Begg, is an important one for human rights defenders on both sides of the Atlantic and beyond. Readers outside the UK may be puzzled by the amount of attention we give below to Cageprisoners, a relatively small nonprofit. Cageprisoners is important not only because it has been accepted as a human rights partner by organizations including Amnesty International, the Center for Consitutional Rights, and Reprieve. In their joint campaign to close Guantanamo and try to restore the balance between security and civil liberties, we believe that these organizations, particularly Amnesty International, ended up not only defending prisoners' rights but accepting parts of the ideological framework of the Muslim Right.[45] In the next section, we will demonstrate why we think Cageprisoners is not a human rights organization as it claims, but a public relations group for jihadis and an unsuitable partner for human rights work. We hope to illustrate the way that close reading and examination of the public record, combined with background research, can enable activists to distinguish between defenders of universal human rights and those who use the language of human rights to disguise a different political agenda.

---

[45] Tax, op. cit.

CAGEPRISONERS:
A CASE STUDY

THE STORY OF MOAZZAM BEGG

Moazzam Begg is a British citizen who took his family to live in Afghanistan in 2001 because he supported the Taliban. After 9/11, he and his family went to Pakistan. On 31 January 2002, he was detained by Pakistan and US security forces and held for a year in Bagram prison in Afghanistan and two more in Guantanamo without being charged. During his imprisonment at Bagram, Begg was questioned by the FBI and signed a confession admitting he "was armed and prepared to fight alongside the Taliban and al-Qaeda against the US." He says he did so after being hog-tied and beaten as he listened "to the sound of a woman screaming next door I'm told or am led to believe is my wife."[46] Begg maintains that this confession, in which he admitted being associated with al-Qaeda, was extracted under torture and fear of death; this charge was investigated four times by various US governmental agencies and they all dispute it. This will be discussed later.

While Begg's confession to the FBI is part of the public record, we have not based the following story on it since he says it was extracted under duress. Our narrative is based on his book

---

[46] "Julian Assange Interviews Moazzam Begg and Asim Qureshi for *The World Tomorrow*". Cageprisoners. 15 May 2012. www.cageprisoners. com/our-work/interviews/item/4202-julian-assanges-the-world-tomorrow-cageprisoners-surviving-guantanamo; Golden, T. 2006. "Jihadist or Victim: Ex-Detainee Makes a Case", *The New York Times*, 15 June.

Enemy Combatant (2006), co-authored by Victoria Brittain, as well as interviews and his handwritten signed statement to the US Military Tribunal, which he does not dispute.

Moazzam Begg was born in Birmingham in 1968 to a family of Indian Muslims. Begg's father was a bank manager, and he graduated from Wolverhampton University. He became interested in Islam during a family trip to Pakistan and Saudi Arabia and, in late 1993, during the war against the Soviets, went back to Pakistan and crossed the border into Afghanistan. There he met various mujahideen and visited a training camp run by Pakistanis from Jamaat-i-Islami[47] to aid those fighting in Kashmir. He was particularly impressed by the "emir" of this camp, who told him:

> To me jihad is like a drug I'm allowed to take, and I always come back for more. I feel I have fulfilled my purpose in life when I come to the defence of the oppressed ... As long as Muslim lands are occupied I have vowed to fight for their liberation. It is my duty as a Muslim, as a Pakistani and as a human. Death in this path does not frighten me – I welcome it, with open arms. One of our brothers, martyred years ago, in these very mountains against Rūs [Russia], said something I will never forget: "Much of mankind has chosen life as a path to death, but I have chosen death as a path to life."[48]

Begg's 1993 visit to the training camp for mujahideen moved him deeply: "The Afghan visit was a life-changing experience for me.

---

[47] Jamaat e Islami is a far right Islamist party in Pakistan and Bangladesh. Some of its Bangladesh leaders are currently on trial for war crimes committed during the war of independence. Pakistani Jamaat e Islami promotes jihad against the Indian government in Kashmir.
[48] Begg, op. cit., p. 57.

No few days have ever affected me like that. I had met men who seemed to me exemplary in their faith and self-sacrifice, and seen a world that awed and inspired me."[49]

Thus motivated, Begg decided to help the Bosnians in the Yugoslav civil war. He made a number of trips to Bosnia under the auspices of the Convoy of Mercy, an Islamist charity organized by Asad Khan, an electrical engineer from Finchley, to avert what he described as "Europe's Muslim Holocaust".[50] Horrified by what he saw, Begg briefly joined the Bosnian Army Foreign Volunteer Force. In 1999, he also attempted to travel to Chechnya to join the Islamist insurgency there, but was unable to gain entry.[51]

At some point along this trajectory, Begg decided he was not cut out to be a fighter[52] and could be more useful in other ways. He returned to Birmingham in 1998 and, with a partner, opened a bookstore called Maktabah al Ansaar. Their motive was "to make enough money to support our families, to give some of the profits to charity and to educate people about Islam."[53] Begg makes the bookshop sound like an innocuous do-it-yourself operation: "We produced some of our own publications translated from Arabic, which is something I rather enjoyed doing. I also designed a large poster for children that taught Arabic letters."[54]

In fact, the Maktabah al Ansar bookshop was one of the most important publishers and distributors of salafi-jihadi political

---

[49] Begg, op. cit., p. 53.
[50] "The Bosnian War". 20 August 2012. www.salaam.co.uk.
[51] Begg, op. cit., pp. 83-7.
[52] Guttenplan, D. D. and M. Margaronis. 2010. "Who Speaks for Human Rights?" *The Nation*, 5 April.
[53] Begg, op. cit., p. 75.
[54] *Ibid.*

material in the UK,[55] and was raided three times by British authorities.[56] In 1999, while Begg was in charge, it commissioned and published a definitive book, *The Army of Madinah in Kashmir*, by Dhiren Barot, describing his military activities in Kashmir. The book, which uses the term "defensive jihad", contains descriptions of the jihad in Kashmir, an analysis of the Government of Pakistan, instructions on how to find jihadi camps and justifications for carrying out acts of terrorism in the West. A note at the end celebrates the 1999 hijacking of Indian Airlines flight 814 by a group of Pakistani mujahideen, during which a passenger was stabbed to death.[57] Dhiren Barot is also the author of a manual on how to make bombs from ordinary household materials; the manual was found on an al-Qaeda laptop captured in Pakistan, along with Barot's reports of a reconnaissance trip to the US in 2000 to survey potential targets for attack. Barot was tried in the UK, pled guilty to charges of planning to use car bombs and a radioactive "dirty bomb" on various financial institutions in the US, and was sentenced to thirty years for conspiracy to murder.[58]

It is well known that bookstores and publishers like Maktabah al Ansaar played an important role in the growth of jihadi movements in the 1990s. A recent description of a similar bookstore in Indonesia shows the way such bookstores and publishing houses function as centralizing nodes of radical Islamist activity:

---

[55] Hosenball, M. 2004. "Terrorism – Barnes and Noble It's Not", *Newsweek*, 6 December.
[56] habibi, "Martyrdom for Maktabah", *Harry's place*, 4 February 2010. http://hurryupharry.org/2010/02/04/end-of-the-line-for-maktabah/.
[57] habibi, "Begg, Barot, and Kashmir", *Harry's place*, 9 February 2010. http://hurryupharry.org/2010/02/09/begg-barot-and-kashmi.
[58] United States Nuclear Regulatory Commission. May 2007. "Backgrounder on Dirty Bombs". http://www.nrc.gov/reading- rm/ doc-collections/fact-sheets/dirty-bombs-bg.html.
[59] Gelling, P. 2009. "Radical Books Raise Fears in Indonesia of Spread of Mililtants' Ideas", *The New York Times*, 8 February.

At a small, back-street bookstore here, the young employees, wearing matching green skullcaps and sporting wispy chin beards, stock books with titles like, "Waiting for the Destruction of Israel" and "Principles of Jihad". They work quietly, listening to the voice of a firebrand Islamic preacher playing on the store's sound system, his sermon peppered with outbursts of machine-gun fire. Another young man, a customer, sifts through a pile of DVDs that chronicle the conflicts in Chechnya, Afghanistan and Sudan. T-shirts, stickers and pins on sale at the back of the store are emblazoned with slogans like, "Support Your Local Mujahideen" and "Taliban All-Stars". The jihadi books at the store, which is called Arofah, have been made available by a small but growing group of publishers in and around Solo, a commercial city known as a bastion of conservative Islam. Many of the publishers openly support the ideological goals of Jemaah Islamiyah, a banned Southeast Asia terrorist network that has been implicated in most of the major terrorist bombings in Indonesia ...

"The most interesting aspect is what the publishing operations reveal about the overlapping networks binding Jemaah Islamiyah together," said Sidney R. Jones, an analyst with the non-profit International Crisis Group in Jakarta, Indonesia's capital ... She notes that Solo is not only the base for the publishers, but also the site of Pesantren al-Mukmin, an Islamic boarding school that has educated some of the country's most notorious extremists. Some of the publishers have taught at the school, and Abu Bakar Bashir, a militant Islamic cleric who helped found the school, originally conceived of the idea of opening publishing houses in Solo that could specialize in books on Islam, Ms. Jones said. Mr. Bashir served time in prison on conspiracy charges in several bombings, including those in Bali.[59]

Moazzam Begg's bookstore Maktabah al Ansaar was this kind of centre, a strategic node for dissemination of works by, among others, Abdullah Azzam and Osama Bin Laden, the founders of al-Qaeda, and Ayman al Zawahiri, its current leader. The bookshop became a gathering place for people interested in jihad, the kind of place where an aspiring militant could meet people who would help him get to Afghanistan. To add to the attraction, one of Begg's employees was a member of the Algerian Islamic Armed Group, one of the organizations responsible for the campaign of fundamentalist terror in Algeria in the 1990s.[60] The bookstore was a centre for debate about jihad, and how and when it should be waged, and Begg came to believe that, however some might interpret it, "until modern times, the majority of Muslims (and the non-Muslims they used it on) always understood jihad as warfare."[61]

One of the things Begg particularly liked about running the bookstore was the interesting people he met. "In the bookshop I used to hear a lot about Afghanistan from people who were going back and forth regularly, and one of them told me about a school project he had initiated in Kabul. He was a Palestinian, Rami, based in Britain. He asked whether I was willing to help."[62]

Although Begg does not mention this in *Enemy Combatant*, one can deduce from an interview he did for Cageprisoners[63] that his friend Rami was none other than Mahmoud Abu Rideh, a leading

---

[60] UK Home Office. "Appeal No: SC/6/2002". www.unhcr.org/refworld/pdfid/4990287a2.pdf.
[61] Begg, op. cit., pp. 80-81.
[62] Begg, op. cit., p. 90.
[63] "Moazzam Begg Interviews Mahmoud Abu Rideh". Cagerisoners. 17 June 2008. www.cageprisoners.com/our-work/interviews/item/139-moazzam-begg-interviews-mahmoud-abu-rideh.

figure in al-Qaeda who functioned as its moneyman. Abu Rideh had spent many years in Pakistan and Afghanistan working with Abdullah Azzam and Osama bin Laden's Afghan Services Bureau – he is said to have moved money around Afghanistan concealed in a plaster cast on his leg. He came to the UK in 1995, where he received indefinite leave to remain but was arrested in December 2001 on charges of being a supporter of terrorist groups – he had allegedly raised £100,000 for al-Qaeda in two years, funneling the money through the Arab Bank in London's Park Lane. Another of his bank accounts, at the Wimbledon branch of HSBC was called "Islamic Services Bureau – Treasurer's Account". After years in prison and under a control order, Abu Rideh left the UK in late 2009 and returned to Afghanistan, where it was reported that he had become a "martyr" in December 2010, killed by a drone strike.[64]

Begg was impressed by Abu Rideh's stories of all the good he could accomplish in Afghanistan, building wells and setting up schools, and "began to feel that this was something I really wanted to get involved in ... The simple fact of the cost of living there weighed with me, too. Many people told me that we could live in the best area of Kabul for less than £100 a month and gradually, the idea of uprooting the family and going there to live took hold of me."[65]

Begg had married in 1995 and by this time had three children. In July 2001, he and his family moved to Afghanistan. It seemed like a good time; the Taliban had consolidated its control and the civil war was over. He went to Afghanistan, as he later told US interrogators, because, "I wanted to live in an Islamic

---

[64] Gardham, D. and P. Swami. 2010. "British Al-Qaeda Refugee Killed in Afghanistan", *Daily Telegraph*, 16 December.
[65] Begg, op. cit., pp. 91-2.

state – one that was free from the corruption and despotism of the rest of the Muslim world … The Taliban were better than anything Afghanistan has had in the past 25 years."[66] Begg's friend, Shaker Aamer, along with his wife and children, soon joined him.[67]

Begg and his supporters have referred to his activities in building schools for both boys and girls as evidence that neither he nor the Taliban discriminated against women. Says Fahad Ansari, an active writer on the Cageprisoners website, "The fact is that before Begg was kidnapped, he was involved in the building of, the setting up of and the running of a school for girls in Afghanistan during the time of the Taliban."[68] In his handwritten testimony at Guantanamo, Begg says, "My aim in Afghanistan was to continue [to offer] social value and assistance to those less fortunate than myself," particularly by establishing a school.[69]

> The plan was to expand both boys and girls schools to incorporate secondary education – and a link to the Kabul University. We collected books, funds and stationery; together with computers, classroom furniture and playground apparatus. I was very excited with the project after having received photographs of the school students; playgrounds; classrooms; school buses; outings, etc. I also received copies of curricula, syllabi, and reports from teachers and the headmaster …

---

[66] Begg, op. cit., p. 214.
[67] Verkaik, R. 2010. "Shaker Aamer, Guantanamo's last British detainee", *The Independent*, 3 March.
[68] Ansari, F. "The Problem with Gita". 2 February 2010. http://old. cageprisoners.com/ articles.php?id=31054.
[69] US Department of Defense. 2004. "Response to Tribunal Process – Begg, Moazzam". 15 September. pdf. Retrieved 19 July 2011.

Though the girls' school was not authorized by th strict Taliban regime, I still enrolled my own daughter at the school, and my son at the boys – though he was still too young.[70]

Similarly, interviewed by Begg, Abu Rideh says, "We worked together to build that school ... for girls in a place where the rest of the world was saying that the Taliban did not allow female education, when in fact Muslims were helping to set up schools, like yourself, for girls in Afghanistan."[71]

But how could this be, when the Taliban did not allow education for girls over the age of eight and had closed down all the girls' schools in Afghanistan? The answer is that the school was not for Afghan girls. It was a school set up by al-Qaeda's treasurer and Begg for the children of foreign jihadis, including his own. Abu Rideh himself said the fathers of children at the school were "some of the world's most wanted men."[72] Begg's work in Afghanistan was hardly a disinterested act of social service to advance the education of women.

Begg's decision to move his family to Kabul proved to be poorly timed. Two months after he arrived, al-Qaeda attacked the World Trade Center and Pentagon and in October the US started bombing Kabul, Kandahar and Jalalabad, where al-Qaeda had a training camp. Begg's wife and children evacuated to Logar, a town on the Pakistani border, but Begg himself kept going in and out of Kabul "to check on our house, buy food, and get news."[73] He had made friends with some Pakistani jihadis

---

[70] *Ibid.*
[71] "Begg Interviews Abu Rideh", op. cit.
[72] Gardham and Swami, op. cit.
[73] Begg, op. cit., p. 100.
[74] Begg, op. cit., p. 97.

who took him to the front lines.[74] He was with them on the day he heard Kabul had fallen. At this point, Begg's story and the time frame become vague and confusing: he couldn't evacuate through Kabul; some of the Pakistani jihadis wanted to go to Jalalabad; others said they would take him to Logar but the road was blocked; they got lost; they ended up in the mountains and, after two days, finally crossed into Pakistan through mountain roads full of men with guns, and exited via some caves.

In other words, he escaped through the Tora Bora Mountains, which lie east of Kabul and close to the Pakistani border. They contain a complex of caves used in the war with the Soviets that were taken over by Osama bin Laden and used as al-Qaeda headquarters. The battle of Tora Bora was in part a delaying action to gain time for Osama bin Laden and most of the other al-Qaeda people to escape through the caves. In his handwritten testimony at Guantanamo, Begg says only that he and his friends abandoned their vehicle for fear of highwaymen and hired a guide to take them over the mountains into Pakistan. "Interrogators have claimed my route was through Tora Bora. I do not know what the place was called nor did I stay to find out. I did meet other people evacuating this route – some may have been fighters – or just armed locals, as is common there."[75]

In mid-November 2001, the Northern Alliance took Jalalabad and allowed a reporter, Jack Kelley from *USA Today*, to poke around the al-Qaeda training camp at Darunta. He reported:

> Plastic explosives, timing devices and sketches of the best places to hide a bomb on an airplane filled the

---

[75] US Department of Defense. op. cit.

files of Osama bin Laden's terrorist training camps near here. Gas masks, cyanide and recipes for biological agents lined the shelves of his chemical weapons laboratory ... In another drawer were several fake visa and immigration stamps, one purporting to be from the Pakistani Embassy in Rome and another from the Tajikistan Consulate in Islamabad, Pakistan. There was also a photocopy of a money transfer requesting that a London branch of Pakistan's Habib Bank, AG Zurich, credit the account of an individual identified as Moazzam Begg in Karachi for an unspecified sum of money. US and Pakistani officials say they do not know who Begg is but will try to find him.[76]

A month and a half later, on 31 January 2002, Pakistani and American officers arrested Begg at his Islamabad home and held him as an "enemy combatant". After three weeks, he was moved to Afghanistan and confined in the US army base in Bagram for a year, where he says he signed a confession for the FBI under duress; he was then transferred to Guantanamo, where he spent two more years, much of it in solitary confinement. He was never formally charged; nor was he allowed access to a lawyer for most of the time he was imprisoned.

It should be noted that, while some US prisoners were held by the CIA in "black sites" and subjected to torture, not all prisoners were treated the same way. The Department of Defense conducted three separate investigations into Begg's allegations and interviewed thirty witnesses; its 2005 report says: "Many of the witnesses interviewed by the Army investigators said that Begg cooperated with military interrogators by assisting with translations, that Begg received comforts such as reading

---

[76] "Bin Laden's camps teach curriculum of carnage", *USA Today*, 26 November 2001.

and writing materials and that Begg never complained about mistreatment while he was at Bagram."[77] The Office of the Inspector General of the US Department of Justice, an investigative body set up to "detect and deter waste, fraud, abuse, and misconduct in DOJ programmes and personnel,"[78] looked into Begg's claims of mistreatment by the FBI and concluded that they had no basis in fact and that, on the contrary, the FBI strategy was to try to coax him to plead guilty. They reported that Begg went over his confession after it was typed to make sure that it was accurate, and then initialed his changes so that it was clear he had signed off on them:

> The OIG reviewed a copy of Begg's signed statement, dictated 13 February 2002. The statement is eight single-spaced pages, and signed by Begg, Bell, Harrelson, and two DOD Criminal Investigative Division agents. Begg's signed statement indicates, among other things, that Begg sympathized with the cause of al-Qaeda, attended terrorist training camps in Afghanistan, Pakistan, and England so he could assist in waging global jihad against enemies of Islam, including Russia and India; associated with and assisted several prominent terrorists and supporters of terrorists and discussed potential terrorist acts with them; recruited young operatives for the global jihad; and provided financial support for terrorist training camps.

---

[77] Office of the Inspector General, US Department of Justice. 2008. "A Review of the FBI's Involvement in and Observations of Detainee Interrogations in Guantanamo Bay, Afghanistan, and Iraq", May, p. 268. Note that most accusations of torture by US personnel have been directed at the CIA, not the FBI. The DOJ document does not state clearly whether or not the CIA was involved in Begg's interrogation at Bagram.
[78] Office of the Inspector General. US Department of Justice. www.justice.gov/oig/.

Notations that appear to be Begg's handwritten initials appear at the beginning and the end of each paragraph of the statement. The statement has additions and deletions that are also initialed. These include both minor and substantive changes. For example, on the first page Begg apparently corrected the spelling of one of his aliases, changed "handguns" to "handgun", and deleted "hand" in front of "grenades". On page 3, Begg apparently changed the statement "I am unsure of the exact amount of money sent to terrorist training camps of the many years I helped fund the camps", by replacing the word "many" with the words "couple of". On p. 4 he added the following sentence apparently for purposes of explanation of his conduct: "This was to help the Kurds in Iraq."[79]

All this raises important questions. So does Begg's memoir, in which his persona is that of a good-hearted, wide-eyed innocent who bumbles his way through world-historical events without really understanding what's going on. As Jonathan Raban said in a review of the book, "Like many inept first-person narrators (and aspiring politicians), he attributes to himself a degree of earnest naiveté that doesn't square well with his story. A few bland generalities about injustice, conscience and self-defence are all we are allowed to hear about the detailed politics and theology of radical Islamism, which is a pity."[80] The reader may wonder how a man this naive could have built a world-class jihadi bookstore and become a major political spokesman and commentator after his release from Guantanamo.

---

[79] Office of the Inspector General 2008, op. cit. pp. 275-6.
[80] Raban, J. 2006. "The Prisoners Speak", *New York Review of Books*, 5 October.

During the time that Begg was imprisoned, many UK writers and political activists protested against US human rights violations at Guantanamo. Among them were left wing journalist Victoria Brittain, formerly an editor at *The Guardian*, and novelist Gillian Slovo. Together they wrote a documentary play, *Guantanamo: Honour Bound to Defend Freedom*, which premiered at the Tricycle Theater in London in May 2004, transferred to the West End, and subsequently played in New York. Moazzam Begg is featured in the play as a British prisoner who loses his mind due to his harsh confinement.[81]

The Labour government pressed for the release of British prisoners held in Guantanamo and in January 2005, despite the objections of US intelligence, President Bush released Begg and three others as a favour to Tony Blair.[82] Upon his return to the UK, Begg began to work with Victoria Brittain on a memoir, *Enemy Combatant*, which was published in March 2006 and contains a full account of his ordeal in Bagram and Guantanamo. Even before the book was published, Begg was a media figure; the memoir further increased his visibility as one who could speak about Guantanamo from personal experience. He published op-eds in *The Guardian* and became a frequent commentator and public speaker, much in demand at antiwar events and on platforms with Amnesty International, Reprieve and the Center for Constitutional Rights. In fact, in Gita Sahgal's words, Begg became "Britain's most famous supporter of the Taliban."[83]

And he remained its supporter. *Enemy Combatant* is a consistent

---

[81] Whittaker, R. 2004. "Guantanamo – Honor Bound to Defend Freedom, Tricycle, London", *The Independent*, 30 May.
[82] Golden, op. cit.
[83] Bright, M. 2010. "Amnesty International, Moazzam Begg, and the Bravery of Gita Sahgal", *The Spectator*, 7 February.

apologia for the Taliban; any second thoughts are implicit, muted, confined to comparatively minor issues, and with significant qualification. Begg's attitude toward the Taliban is more elegiac than critical: "When I went to Afghanistan, I believed that the Taliban had made some modest progress – in social justice and in upholding pure, old-style Islamic values forgotten in many Islamic countries. After September 11th that life was destroyed."[84] In 2009, Moazzam Begg became Director of Cageprisoners, founded as a website in 2003. Its visibility increased when Begg came on board, though Cageprisoners also has a number of other prominent members and patrons, including Victoria Brittain, Andy Worthington, Yvonne Ridley, Asim Qureshi, Fahad Ansari of the Islamic Human Rights Commission, and, most recently, Lauren Booth, the sister-in-law of ex-Prime Minister Tony Blair and a convert to Islam.

THE RULE OF LAW VS. "FREE THE PRISONERS"

Cageprisoners' website states that it "exists solely to raise awareness of the plight of the prisoners at Guantanamo Bay and other detainees held as part of the War on Terror."[85] It defines itself as having an "Islamic ethos" and says this means it can be more effective than other organizations in helping these prisoners because it "bears in mind the needs of the Muslim communities."[86]

Cageprisoners also calls itself "a human rights organization" with a vision "to see a return to the respect of those fundamental

---

[84] Begg, op. cit., p. 381.
[85] Cageprisoners, "About Us". www.cageprisoners.com/about-us.
[86] *Ibid.*

norms which transcend religion, societies and political theories. It is the vision of Cageprisoners that abuse of individuals and demonization of societies be eradicated completely and that respect for human rights is unequivocally promoted globally."[87]

There seems to be a contradiction here. For Cageprisoners to qualify as a human rights organization, it would have to be willing to defend universality and indivisibility. That means it would have to stand up for equal rights for women, gays, and religious minorities within Islam. A commitment to universality is the very definition of a human rights organization, as is the recognition that human rights are indivisible; you cannot choose some rights and disregard others.

But, judging by the cases Cageprisoners highlights, its principle of selection has less to do with universal, indivisible human rights than with the desire to support activists in jihadi networks. In fact, rather than doing human rights work, the organization is obeying the salafist injunction to "free the prisoners", i.e., free those Muslims who have been jailed for making war on unbelievers and invaders of "Muslim lands". It has no interest in any other Muslim prisoners. And it does not distinguish between prisoners like those at Guantanamo whose rights to habeas corpus and due process of law have been violated and prisoners who have been tried and found guilty in a normal courtroom setting. Gita Sahgal examined the Cageprisoners website thoroughly in 2010 and 2011. She concluded:

> Careful examination of the Cageprisoners website shows that their goal was to obtain the release of such [salafi-jihadi] prisoners, rather than simply affording them fair trial and punishment by a properly constituted

---

[87] *Ibid.*

court. So while one section of the website appears to work within human rights standards, others are more clearly dedicated to imposing a religious obligation to "Free the Prisoners" who are seen as suffering for their faith. Supporters such as Imams are asked to "give fatwa (legal verdicts) explaining to your congregation the obligations of Muslims towards their unjustly detained brethren around the world, and the punishment for abandoning them." Supporting prisoners in this way is not simply an act of charity, but a form of religious support towards their theo-political goals.[88]

To "free the prisoners" is a religious obligation in salafi-jihadi theology. For instance, in *The Defence of Muslim Lands*, Abdullah Azzam says:

> Defensive jihad consists of expelling unbelievers from our territory. This is an individual duty, indeed the most important of all individual duties, in the following cases: 1) when unbelievers enter one of the Muslim territories; 2) when two armies meet and exchange blows; 3) when the imam mobilizes individuals or a group: then they must gather to fight; 4) when unbelievers imprison Muslims.[89]

One could almost say that the phrase "free the prisoners" functions like a code used to alert salafi-jihadi sympathizers while passing unnoticed by liberal readers, who assume that Cageprisoners means support for due process of law.

---

[88] Sahgal, G. July, 2011. "Dissent vs. Incitement?" *Infochange*. www.centreforsecularspace.org/?q=resources.
[89] Azzam, op. cit.

In an article for *Arches Quarterly*,[90] Moazzam Begg links military jihad to freeing the prisoners and describes both as obligatory for believers:

> By consensus of the Islamic schools of thought, jihad becomes an individual obligation, like prayer and fasting, on Muslim men and women when their land is occupied by foreign enemies. That obligation extends to neighbouring lands until the enemy has been expelled. If the whole body of believers abandon it, they are in a state of sin; if enough of them do it to complete the task, they are absolved. Jihad using wealth is also obligatory in securing the release of Muslim prisoners. Imam Malik said: 'If a Muslim is held as a prisoner of war ... it is obligatory on others to secure his release, even if it requires all the Muslims' wealth.'[91]

Anwar al-Awlaki, a leader of al-Qaeda in the Arabian Peninsula who was killed by a CIA drone attack in September 2011, also stressed the hadith's command to "Free the prisoner". In his *44 Ways to Support Jihad*, al-Awlaki interpreted this to mean all Muslims who are prisoners of war, regardless of what they have done and whether or not they have received a fair trial.

Similarly, Cageprisoners' principles explicitly state: "It is not only the right to a fair trial that Cageprisoners promotes, rather the morality of the law. Thus even though national legislation in

---

[90] *Arches Quarterly* is published by the Cordoba Foundation, which was founded and is headed by Anas Altakriti, formerly President of the Muslim Association of Britain (affiliated with the Muslim Brotherhood) and a member of the Respect Party.
[91] Begg, M. 2008. "Jihad and Terrorism – A War of the Words", *Arches Quarterly*, II.1, Summer 2008, p. 20.

various jurisdictions may be given a veneer of legality, in reality they go against the conscience of the law. Thus our understanding of due process goes to the very heart of the counter-terrorism policies that are implemented, whether legally or illegally."[92]

What exactly does this mean? Is this an example of "double discourse", where words mean one thing to Western liberals and another to Islamists? Does Cageprisoners mean that national counter-terrorism legislation may have "a veneer of legality" but is illegitimate because it goes against "the morality of the law?" In other words, laws that set limitations on "defensive jihad" are illegitimate? Or are some counter-terrorism laws legitimate, and others not? What about laws that outlaw incitement to murder in pursuit of freeing "Muslim lands?" Who decides which laws are legitimate and which ones are not? According to what criteria? Do people in Cageprisoners believe that their understanding of "the morality of the law" overrides the laws of the UK and other countries? What is their approach to the rule of law, and why is their language so ambiguous?

The whole structure of human rights is based on the rule of law, as the Universal Declaration says in its preamble: "...it is essential, if man is not to be compelled to have recourse, as a last resort, to rebellion against tyranny and oppression, that human rights should be protected by the rule of law."[93] A group that explicitly disregards the rule of law cannot be considered a human rights group.

In July 2012, the Cageprisoners website listed nine individuals as the subjects of major campaigns: Babar Ahmad, Aafia Siddiqui, Shaker Aamer, Abu Mu'sab al-Suri, Abu Zubaydah, Iban al-

---

[92] Cageprisoners, "About Us", op. cit.
[93] Office of the United Nations High Commissioner for Human Rights, op. cit.

Shaykh al-Libi, Ravel Mingazov, Hussain Alsamamra and Omar Khadr. Other prisoners Cageprisoners has campaigned for in the past include Anwar al-Awlaki, Ali al-Timimi, Khalid Sheikh-Mohammed, Abu Hamza and Abu Qatada. Some of these are indeed people who were detained unlawfully at Guantanamo or in CIA black sites. Others were brought to trial in various countries, found guilty and sentenced. Some fought a long battle against extradition to the US from Britain. A brief look at a few of these cases shows the range of issues involved:

Babar Ahmad[94] was deported to the US in October 2012 after all legal appeals to keep him in the UK were exhausted. He had been held without trial since 1994. While in prison in Britain, he sued the police for assault and won a significant monetary award. The US has accused him of operating www.azzam.com, a pro-Chechen and pro-Taliban website. A search of his house produced a floppy disk with details of the movements of the US Fifth Fleet through the Straits of Hormuz, saying it would be vulnerable to rocket attack at that time. He has been the subject of a major Cageprisoners campaign.

Aafia Siddiqui,[95] a Pakistani neuroscientist with degrees from Brandeis University in Massachusetts and the Massachusetts Institute of Technology (MIT), was a Muslim student activist in the Boston area until the 9/11 attacks on New York and Washington. Shortly thereafter, she left the US for Pakistan

---

[94] CP Editor. "Babar Ahmad". Cageprisoners. 10 August 2010. www.cageprisoners.com/our-work/focus-campaigns/item/431-babar-ahmad; "Act Now! Last Chance to Stop the Extradition of Babar Ahmad". 4 July 2010. www.cageprisoners.com/our-work/alerts/item/4549-act-now-last-chance-to-stop-the-extradition-of-babar-ahmad.
[95] CP Editor. "Aafia Siddiqui". Cageprisoners. 1 September 2010. www.cageprisoners.com/our-work/focus-campaigns/item/199-aafia-siddiqui.

with her children. Her first husband told the journalist Declan Walsh that he divorced her because "...she was so pumped up about jihad."[96] After the divorce Siddiqui married a nephew of Khalid Shaikh-Mohammed, a top al-Qaeda operative, who apparently named her as an associate after his arrest and torture in 2003. The FBI put out a warrant for her arrest and she disappeared. There are contested versions of where she spent the next five years. Some, including her first husband, think she went underground with her three young children, possibly with the cooperation of Pakistani intelligence. Her supporters believe she and her children were being held in Bagram. She re-emerged in Afghanistan in 2008 and was arrested. The next day, according to the US, she was wounded in a firefight with US soldiers at the police station where she was being held, and was taken to Bagram for treatment. She was then flown to New York, where she was charged with attempted murder and armed assault on US employees rather than any terrorism offenses. She received a trial by jury in 2010, and was convicted and sentenced to 86 years in prison. Her case is a *cause celebre* in Pakistan, where she is seen as a "daughter of the nation" and the government has called for her repatriation.

Shaker Aamer,[97] a British resident born in Saudi Arabia and friend of Moazzam Begg's who followed him to Kabul, was captured in Afghanistan and has been held in Guantanamo without being charged for over ten years, accused of having led a detachment of al-Qaeda fighters at the Battle of Tora Bora. The British government says it is lobbying for his release and Cageprisoners has campaigned energetically on his behalf, pointing out that he has been cleared for release by the US

---

[96] Walsh, D. 2009. "The Mystery of Dr. Aafia Siddiqui". *The Guardian*, 9 November.
[97] CP Editor. "Shaker Aamer". Cageprisoners. 26 July 2010. www.cageprisoners.com/our-work/focus-campaigns/item/197-shaker-aamer.

authorities. The anomaly here is that the accusations against Aamer come partly from testimony by another Guantanamo inmate who, according to recent Wikileaks evidence, was none other than Moazzam Begg himself. An article in the *Wall Street Journal* states:

> In a US Department of Defense memorandum released by WikiLeaks, I have uncovered another, especially devastating source who spoke out against Mr. Aamer in Guantanamo. "UK558" described Mr. Aamer as a "recruiter" for al-Qaeda. He outlined how Mr. Aamer and he traveled to meet members of a European al-Qaeda cell in 2000, and how Mr. Aamer fought in Bosnia under the leadership of Abu Zubayr al-Haili, a senior al-Qaeda figure. "UK558" talked of the training in AK-47s and rocket-propelled grenades Mr. Aamer received. "UK558" is the Defense Department memorandum's code-name for none other than Moazzam Begg. Back in the U.K., Mr. Begg consistently calls for Mr. Aamer's release. He has said that it is Mr. Aamer's "personal character and charisma" that keeps him in Guantanamo, "as opposed to anything he has been accused of."[98]

Abu Mu'sab al-Suri,[99] a Syrian jihadi and theoretician, is a major Cageprisoners case, despite the fact that he is not in prison. Before 9/11, he was the facilitator who used to take Western reporters to meet Osama bin Laden in Afghanistan. In 2005, he published "A Call to a Global Islamic Resistance," a treatise arguing that the future of jihad lay in dissolving al-Qaeda's

---

[98] Simcox, R. 2012. "Guantanamo and its Critics", *Wall Street Journal*, 18 January.
[99] CP Editor. "Abu Mus'ab al Suri". Cageprisoners. 12 July 2010. www.cageprisoners.com/our-work/focus-campaigns/item/195-abu-mus%E2%80%99ab-al-suri.

hierarchical structure in favour of small decentralized local cells that would target Western civilians. He said al-Qaeda's leaders had failed to seize on the opportunities opened by the 9/11 attacks and that bin Laden had caught "the disease of screens, flashes, fans and applause." European intelligence agencies and police believe al-Suri drafted the plans for the Madrid train bombings in 2004 and the London attacks of 2005, and also helped plan Abu Musab al-Zarqawi's terror campaign during the Iraq war. The CIA put a $5 million price on al-Suri's head. He was captured in Pakistan in 2005 and turned over to the Syrian government. President Bashar al-Assad released him in December 2011.[100]

Among the other prominent jihadis Cageprisoners has supported are:

Ali al-Timimi, convicted in a US federal court of soliciting others to wage war on the US and helping the Taliban, and sentenced to life imprisonment;[101]

Abu Hamza, the former imam of the Finsbury Park Mosque in London, who made it into a centre for jihadi recruitment, was charged with inciting hatred and solicitation to murder and was deported to the US after all his appeals failed.[102]

---

[100] Samuels, D. 2012. "The New Mastermind of Jihad", *Wall Street Journal*, 12 April.
[101] Silverman, L. "Ali al-Timimi: A Convicted Victim of an Overwhelming Confusion". 16 May 2005. http://old.cageprisoners.com/articles.php?id=7307.
[102] CP Editor. "Interview with Abu Hamza". Cageprisoners. 6 June 2008. http://www.cageprisoners.com/our-work/interviews/item/140-interview-with-abu-hamza; Ansari, F. "Politicisation of the European Court of Human Rights". Cageprisoners. 2 May 2012. www.cageprisoners.com/learn-more/recommended/item/4101-politicisation-of-the-european-court-of-human-rights; Burke, J. "AK-47 training held at London mosque", *The Observer*, 16 February 2004.

Abu Qatada, who has been held without trial in the UK for ten years. Spanish prosecutors called him the spiritual leader of al-Qaeda and Algerian armed groups; typically, Cageprisoners refers to him only as "an Islamic scholar of Palestinian origin".[103]

Khalid Sheikh-Mohammed, who took credit for organizing the 9/11 attacks in an interview with Al Jazeera.[104] He was arrested in 2003 and subjected to "enhanced interrogation techniques" (i.e. tortured by the CIA). He subsequently confessed to other crimes against civilians including organizing the 1993 bombing of the World Trade Center (carried out by his nephew), the Bali nightclub bombing in 2002 and the murder of *Wall Street Journal* reporter, Daniel Pearl, also in 2002.[105] He is being held in Guantanamo and his trial by military commission is currently ongoing.[106]

A deeper understanding of Cageprisoners' relationship to the salafi-jihadi movement and its ideas can be derived from its association with Anwar al-Awlaki.

---

[103] CP Editor. "Abu Qatada: Cageprisoners Calls for Immediate Release". Cageprisoners. 18 January 2012. www.cageprisoners.com/our-work/press-releases/item/3276-abu-qatada-cageprisoners-calls-for-immediate-release-and-fresh-start; Begg, M. "From Bethlehem to Belmarsh: Abu Qatada's Ordeal in Britain". Cageprisoners. 19 April 2012. www.cageprisoners.com/our-work/opinion-editorial/item/4002-from-bethlehem-to-belmarsh-abu-qatada%E2%80%99s-ordeal-in-britain.
[104] Foudra, Y. 2003. "We left out nuclear targets, for now", *The Guardian*, 3 March.
[105] AP. "Al-Qaeda No. 3 Says He Planned 9/11, Other Plots". 15 March 2007. www.msnbc.msn.com/id/17617986/?GT1=9145#. UM1k6LYZ9o5.
[106] McVeigh, K. "9/11 pretrial hearings begin for Khalid Sheikh Mohammed and four others", *The Guardian*, 15 October 2012.

CAGEPRISONERS AND ANWAR AL-AWLAKI

Anwar al-Awlaki, whose *Constants on the Path to Jihad* we have already discussed, was an American citizen targeted for assassination by the US government and made the subject of a 2010 test case by the Center for Constitutional Rights (CCR) and the American Civil Liberties Union (ACLU).[107] He was killed by a US drone attack in Yemen on 30 September 2011 (his sixteen year old son was subsequently killed in another drone attack). In July 2012, the ACLU and CCR filed suit against senior CIA officials for these targeted killings, using only the generic label, a "US citizen", to describe al-Awlaki.[108] According to Chetan Bhatt, al-Awlaki was one of the most extreme of all salafi-jihadi advocates.

> Al-Awlaki is unambiguously associated with the al-Qaeda organization in the Arabian Peninsula. In one of its major English-language publications,[109] al-Awlaki is featured prominently on the cover, and given the honor of writing its special feature and launching a campaign of assassinations and violence against civilians ... Al-Awlaki explicitly calls for a large-scale campaign of assassinations, bombings and arson in the West, against civilians. He names a Seattle cartoonist as "a prime target of assassination". The same feature section contains a list of names of individuals in

---

[107] Greenwald, G. "ACLU, CCR seek to have Obama enjoined from killing Awlaki without due process". *Salon*. 3 August 2010. www.salon.com/2010/08/03/awlaki/.
[108] See case file on "Al-Aulaqi vs. Panetta" at www.ccrjustice.org.
[109] This is *Inspire*, an online publication launched in 2010 and posted on a variety of radical websites.

Denmark, the Netherlands, the US and the UK, with a picture of a gun underneath. Al-Awlaki goes on to say that the campaign of violence should not just be limited to those "active participants" whom he believes have "blasphemed", but should include "government, political parties, the police, the intelligence services, blogs, social networks, the media" and indeed any Western target. The same section of the publication contains detailed instructions for lone operators on how to make a pipe bomb.[110]

In addition to writing for *Inspire*, al-Awlaki was an active email correspondent with many prospective jihadis and appears to have had great influence. When he served as an imam in Falls Church, Virginia, three of the 9/11 hijackers attended his sermons, one of whom moved from San Diego to Virginia when he did.[111] Major Nidal Malik Hasan, the army psychiatrist who killed 13 people in a mass shooting at Fort Hood in November 2009, also attended. Al-Awlaki exchanged many emails with Hasan before the attack and praised his actions afterwards.[112] The 2009 "Christmas Day" or "underwear" bomber, Umar Farouk Abdulmutallab, told the FBI that al-Awlaki was one of his al-Qaeda trainers, helped him plan the attack, and said it was justified in religious terms.[113] In May 2010, Faisal Shahzad, author of the failed Times Square bombing attempt, told the

---

[110] Bhatt, C. 2010. "The Virtues of Violence". Unpublished paper in author's files.
[111] Thornton, K. 2003. "Chance to foil 9/11 plot lost here, report finds", *San Diego Union Tribune*, 25 July.
[112] Esposito, R., M. Cole and B. Ross. "Officials: US Army Told of Hassan's Contacts with al-Qaeda". *ABC World News*, 9 November 2009. http://abcnews.go.com/Blotter/fort-hood-shooter-contact-al-qaeda-terrorists-officials/story?id=9030873.
[113] Meyer, J. 2009. "US-born cleric linked to airline bombing plot", *Los Angeles Times*, 31 December.

FBI that he was inspired by al-Awlaki and had linked up with him via the Pakistani Taliban on the internet.[114] That same month, after being radicalized by al-Awlaki's online sermons, Roshonara Choudhry stabbed former British Cabinet Minister Stephen Timms.[115]

Cageprisoners had a long relationship with al-Awlaki, whom they refer to as an "Imam".[116] Quotations from his speeches, as well as images of him, have appeared regularly and prominently in Cageprisoner videos. Moazzam Begg was the first person to interview al-Awlaki after his release from a Yemeni prison in 2007. The audio interview, dated 31 December 2007, was widely promoted online. The tone is one of great respect and deference and Begg refers to him as a "Muslim scholar of Yemeni heritage".[117] In September 2008 and August 2009, Cageprisoners promoted al-Awlaki as the keynote speaker at

---

[114] Esposito, E., C. Vlasto and C. Cuomo. "Sources: Shahzad Had Contact With Awlaki, Taliban Chief, and Mumbai Mastermind". *ABC World News*, 6 May 2010. http://abcnews.go.com/Blotter/faisal-shahzad-contact-awlaki-taliban-mumbai-massacre-mastermind/story?id=10575061.
[115] Seamark, M. 2010. "Curse the judge, shout fanatics, as Muslim girl who knifed MP smiles as she gets life", *Daily Mail*, 5 November.
[116] In fact, al-Awlaki's relationship with them goes back to 2003, when Moazzam Begg was still in Guantanamo. The East London Mosque was part of a campaigning coalition called "Stop Police Terror", which later grew into the organization Cageprisoners. One of the sponsors of the campaign, and a speaker at its event at the ELM on 26 December 2003, was Anwar al-Awlaki, who advised attendees not to cooperate with the police. See Lucy Lips. "East London Mosque: When in Trouble, Throw Chaff". *Harry's place.* 9 November 2010. http://hurryupharry.org/2010/11/09/east-london-mosque-when-in-trouble-throw-chaff/.
[117] "Moazzam Begg Interviews Imam Anwar Al Awlaki". Cageprisoners. 31 December 2007. http://old.cageprisoners.com/articles php?id=22926. Accessed 23 September 2011. The interview can also be found on Youtube.

its Ramadan fundraising dinners. Since al-Awlaki was denied entry to the UK, his presentation at both events was to be by video. However, the Kensington and Chelsea Borough Council said that the Cageprisoners event could not proceed in their hall if al-Awlaki's video message was shown, so it had to cancel his speeches.

Cageprisoners met with considerable criticism in the press for its support of al-Awlaki, prompting the organization to issue a press release in November 2010 to clarify its relationship to him. According to Cageprisoners, when it invited al-Awlaki to speak at the fundraising events, it was unaware that his book, *44 Ways to Support Jihad*, endorses killing civilians.[118]

However, as previously discussed in Section I, his CD-ROM lectures on *Constants on the Path to Jihad*, published in 2005, make no distinction between killing civilians and non-civilians. *44 Ways to Support Jihad* does have more practical advice on subjects like arms training, physical fitness for urban and guerrilla warfare, financing, defending, protecting and supporting mujahideen, encouraging others to fight jihad, and instilling the love of jihad in children. While expressing unspecified disagreement with "some of the language and sentiments expressed in the document", Cageprisoners describes it as "a theological argument for the support of jihad as a generality rather than having any specific instructions in relation to specific conflicts."[119]

---

[118] "Press release: Cageprisoners and Anwar al-Awlaki – a factual background". Cageprisoners. 5 November 2010. http://www. cageprisoners.com/our-work/press-releases/item/786-press-release-cageprisoners-and-anwar-al-awlaki-%E2%80%93-a-factual-background.
[119] *Ibid.*

A 2011 editorial by Asim Qureshi, Executive Director of Cageprisoners, asserts that his organization did not know al-Awlaki supported killing civilians until he said so in interviews with Al Jazeera in February 2010.[120] At that point, according to Qureshi, Cageprisoners began to distance itself from al-Awlaki: "We did not equivocate on this point and clarified that we could not back such positions as we did not agree with them from a theological perspective – the attacking of civilians is not from Islam." Since then, according to its press release, Cageprisoners has campaigned for al-Awlaki only in terms of his being targeted for assassination by the US and tried in absentia in Yemen.[121]

Still Cageprisoners continues to defend him as a transcendent thinker and to stress their admiration for his early work. According to Asim Quereshi, "The current US administration should reflect on the opportunity that it missed in Anwar al-Awlaki to understand the needs of the Muslim community and engage with it in order to reach a wider audience."[122] Moazzam Begg wrote on 14 January 2010: "He was not a radical 'preacher of hate' by any stretch of the imagination. Whilst teaching Islamic principles in an erudite and articulate way – he neither shied away from talking about the Islamic concept of jihad (in military terms) nor from condemning the September 11 attacks

---

[120] Qureshi, A. "Anwar al-Awlaki, a missed opportunity". 29 September 2010. http://www.cageprisoners.com/our-work/opinion-editorial/item/787-anwar-al-awlaki-a-missed-opportunity. The article cites the al Jazeera interview in which al-Awlaki was asked why he had encouraged Umar Farouk Abdulmuttalab, the "underwear bomber", to try to blow up an airplane en route from Amsterdam to Detroit. He answered that this was legitimate because civilians were responsible for electing President George Bush. "The American people take part in all its government's crimes."
[121] "Press release", op. cit.
[122] Quereshi, op. cit.

and terrorism in general … Cageprisoners never has and never will support the ideology of killing, whether by suicide bombers or B52s, whether that's authorized by Awlaki or by Obama. Neither will we be forced into determining a person's guilt outside a recognized court of law."[123] Here Cageprisoners talks about the need for a trial in a "recognized" court of law even as its mission statement derides a "veneer of legality".

Since we began work on this study, Cageprisoners has changed its website, which used to have a resource section called "Islamic Focus", including pieces from Anwar al-Awlaki's English language blogs calling for military jihad. Now that section is gone. But al-Awlaki's banned speeches to Cageprisoners and Moazzam Begg's interview with him are still up on Youtube.[124]

DOES CAGEPRISONERS AGREE WITH ANWAR AL-AWLAKI?

Moazzam Begg's support for the political ideology of global jihad is consistent and clear; it permeates his post-detention writings and speeches, as well as his book. It is the same politics promoted by Abdullah Azzam in his *Defence of Muslim Lands*: Begg believes that it is legitimate in international law for foreign fighters to make war anywhere in the world in "self defence" of "Muslim lands", and that this is comparable to the right of national self-

---

[123] Begg, M. "Cageprisoners and the Great Underpants Conspiracy". Cageprisoners. 10 January 2010. www.cageprisoners.com/our-work/opinion-editorial/item/113-cageprisoners-and-the-great-underpants-conspiracy.
[124] "Anwar Al Awlaki Beyond Guantanamo Lecture Cageprisoners – Part 1/3", www.youtube.com/watch?v=iRDubjBIF68. Part 2/3, www.youtube.com/watch?v=3seHzvcCwrI. Part 3/3, www.youtube.com/watch?v=Ry9HkbrmaOc.

determination. So does Asim Qureshi, Cageprisoners' Executive Director, as he said during the question and answer session after his 2007 speech at Queen Mary University's Islamic Society in London – though he also tried to give enthusiastic would-be jihadis a dose of realism:

> From the perspective of international law, you can go out there and you can fight right now. There's nothing that stops you from doing so, because the principle of self-determination says that it is the inalienable right of all people to fight against alien occupation, colonial domination and racist regimes ... Now the question is, is it [going abroad to fight] a correct, sensible, pragmatic thing for somebody from the UK to do. That is what is debatable; Islamicly I'm talking about. Are you somebody who is capable of doing something like that for a start? ... In most cases people come back with their tail between their legs because they can't even do it. And that's the truth. I've known people to go out to places like Afghanistan and they came back within a week because they couldn't hack it. That's the reality of the situation. In terms of the law, there's no problem with doing it though, whatsoever. And in terms of Islamicly, of course not.[125]

While Cageprisoners believes it is perfectly legal to become a mujahideen in places like Afghanistan, Palestine, Chechnya and Kashmir, they have differences with al-Qaeda on the subject of "defensive jihad". Osama bin Laden and Anwar al-Awlaki believed it was necessary to carry on armed struggle during this period by attacking civilians in the West. This reading of "defensive jihad" was used to justify 9/11 and 7/7. Cageprisoners, on the other

---

[125] habibi. "Queen Mary and Terrorism". *Harry's place*. 25 February 2011. http://hurryupharry.org/2011/02/25/queen-mary-and-terrorism/.

hand, thinks it is not a good idea to stage attacks in places like London where one is actually living – the response to al-Qaeda's 9/11 attacks did, after all, result in the destruction of the "ideal Muslim society" in Afghanistan. In his *Arches* article, Moazzam Begg says attacks like those of 9/11 and 7/7 are "dishonourable", though he also says that he considers the Western attacks in Afghanistan and Iraq to be far worse.[126]

While Begg may have disagreements with al-Qaeda, he does not dwell on these differences. Instead, he and others in Cageprisoners use a series of rhetorical ploys that function to displace the key issues at stake. They contrast the West's current abhorrence of jihad to previous Western support for the mujahideen during the Cold War and the Soviet invasion of Afghanistan. They compare the Taliban or the Iraqi insurgency to national liberation movements like the ANC or Sinn Fein, implying that, if the latter have become legitimate, why not jihadis? Begg says in his *Arches* piece, "It is not surprising too that Muslims have become angry and have even responded with actions rejected by Islam to unleash their outrage. If resisting the Soviet occupation of Afghanistan was jihad, if the repelling the massacres by the Serbs in Bosnia was jihad, then how can resisting the current occupation of these Muslims lands be anything else?"[127] He goes on to compare the Taliban to the British Home Army in the Second World War.

Such rhetorical strategies are attempts to render acceptable a political ideology whose views of self-defence, war and military engagement are completely different from those of international humanitarian law or the law of armed conflict – and to justify Cageprisoners' definition of itself as a human rights organization.

---

[126] Begg, *Arches Quarterly*, op. cit., p. 22.
[127] *Ibid.*

"NEVER TRUST THE ARTIST, TRUST THE TALE"

When a group is trying to be both a human rights and a salafi-jihadi public relations organization at the same time – or when they are playing a double game and using the language of human rights to cover up a different agenda – mistakes of tone are bound to occur. Such mistakes arise when the protagonists assume their own jihadi worldview is more widely shared than is the case.

One such instance relates to a videogame in which Moazzam Begg was to star as body double for the lead character, an orange jumpsuited prisoner who was supposed to shoot his way out of Guantanamo. The videogame, called *Rendition: Guantanamo*, was to be produced for Xbox by a small Scottish company and targeted at the Middle East market.[128] US right wing pundits found out about the project, however, and made such a fuss that the company cancelled it.[129]

A similar misjudgment was made after the extrajudicial killing of Osama bin Laden by US troops in May 2011. Shortly thereafter Cageprisoners published a would-be satiric piece headlined, "Breaking News: Barack Obama is Dead."[130] Probably believing that the US would release a photo of the dead bin Laden, they

---

[128] "Guantanamo: The XBox Game", *The Telegraph*, 1 May 2009.
[129] "Official Statement Regarding Rendition: Guantanamo". 3 June 2009. www. renditionthegame.com; Huessner, M. "9 Video Games That Went Too Far", *ABC News*, 4 June 2009. http://abcnews.go.com/ Technology/GameOn/story?id=7750809&page=1#.UM566LYZ9o4.
[130] This piece and the picture have been taken off the Cageprisoner's website but they were widely archived and can be found by googling the headline, "Breaking News: Barack Obama is Dead."

ran the piece with a gruesome photo-shopped picture of Obama as a corpse with his head covered in blood and his eyes shot out.

The caption under the picture said, "American War Criminal Barack Obama has been killed by Pakistani security forces in the UK, Prime Minister Hasan Abdullah of Pakistan has said." The article, written by Fahad Ansari, a frequent contributor to the Cageprisoners website, describes a firefight in a compound, explains why Obama was targeted by Pakistan for assassination, and continues: "Pakistani media reports said that the body was cremated at the stake to conform with Christian practice of a dignified burial and to prevent any grave becoming a shrine."

The article and especially the picture provoked so much criticism that Cageprisoners had to take the picture off its website and issue a clarification which, inevitably, accuses critics of Islamophobia:

> The idea of the piece was to highlight the immorality of extrajudicial killings to those who justify and celebrate the assassination of Osama Bin Laden ... It was clear that this was a satirical piece highlighting the fact that the episode raised many questions which were pertinent to the application of the rule of law and international norms and principles. It was not in any way, as some have alleged, a wish or notice of intention. This is a distorted reading of the article and reflective of the Islamophobic lens through which Muslim writers are seen.[131]

---

[131] CP Editor. "Clarification of Cageprisoners piece on the fictional killing of Barak Obama". Cageprisoners. 11 May 2011. www.cageprisoners.com/our-work/opinion-editorial/item/1544-clarification-of-cageprisoners-piece-on-the-killing-of-barack-obama.

In *Studies in Classic American Literature*, D.H. Lawrence writes about the distance between intention and execution, and how often the story that is actually told may belie the purpose of the author: "The artist usually sets out – or used to – to point a moral and adorn a tale. The tale, however, points the other way, as a rule. Two blankly opposing morals, the artist's and the tale's. Never trust the artist. Trust the tale." No one sensitive to tone could mistake Ansari's pleasure in the idea that Obama would get a taste of his own medicine. He voiced similar sentiments in a 2003 article about Guantanamo in which he projected the following response to 9/11 onto a hypothetical Pakistani prisoner:

> Let us try and look at this from the viewpoint of a Pakistani detainee. September 11, 2001 – as you hear about the atrocities committed in the US, you cannot help but feel a little happiness that for once, the hunter has become the hunted. Yes, thousands of innocents perished in the attack but for once, the Americans will feel the pain and anguish felt by victims of American terror around the world from places as far apart as Guatemala to Iraq to Japan. As wrong as it may be, it is difficult to suppress the sentiment of justice being done.[132]

An even less mediated voice can be heard in a speech made by Asim Qureshi, the Executive Director of Cageprisoners, at a rally of Hizb ut-Tahrir on 19 August 2006:[133]

---

[132] Ansari, F. "Guantanamo Bay Prisoners". *Pakistan Monitor*, 29 November 2003. http://pak.mediamonitors.net/content/view/full/253.
[133] Hizb ut-Tahrir is an Islamist organization that works for a global Caliphate and thus has a discriminatory agenda but professes non-violence. It is legal in many countries but banned in Bangladesh, Egypt, Russia and Turkey.

We embrace the mercy. We embrace every single thing that is set upon us and we deal with it because we have no fear. So when we see the example of our brothers and sisters fighting in Chechnya, Iraq, Palestine, Kashmir, Afghanistan then we know where the example lies. When we see Hezbollah defeating the armies of Israel, we know what the solution is and where the victory lies. We know that it is incumbent upon all of us to support the jihad of our brothers and sisters in these countries when they are facing the oppression of the West.[134]

It is impossible for an organization to completely disguise its deepest views. In March, 2011, for instance, a blog by Ayesha Kazmi, a frequent contributor to the Cageprisoners website, deplored the fact that 30 per cent of jihadi terrorist plots thwarted by US Homeland Security were uncovered as a result of tips coming from US Muslims. Kazmi was appalled by

> the permissiveness with which American Muslims treat the whistle-blowing taking place within their communities and inside their mosques. That American Muslims have had to resort to policing their own communities not only speaks to the immense burden placed on them, but the willingness of leaders and communities to unquestionably acquiesce to the established bullying narrative of 'Islam and Muslims are inherently violent and they need to sort themselves out,' and the subsequent pressures on Muslim Americans to root out the extremism and terrorism within their midst ... The facts are true. American Muslims accused and imprisoned because of their

---

[134] Asim Qureshi, Executive Director of Cageprisoners, addresses Hizb ut-Tahrir rally, 19 August 2006: www.youtube.com.

alleged involvement in planning terrorist plots, such as Tarek Mehanna, were tipped off by members in their own community. This is hardly a phenomenon to be applauded and encouraged …"[135]

In other words, Thou Shalt Not Snitch.

SUMMARY

To sum up: Moazzam Begg is the head of Cageprisoners, which calls itself a human rights organization and has been accepted as such by major UK and international human rights groups including the Aire Center, Amnesty International, British Irish Rights Watch, Freedom from Torture, Human Rights Watch, Justice, Liberty, Redress and Reprieve,[136] as well as the US Center for Constitutional Rights.[137] The two donors from which Cageprisoners draws its core support are the Joseph Rowntree Charitable Trust – an organization of pacifist Quakers – and the Roddick Foundation, which funds social justice and human rights causes and was set up by a feminist.

---

[135] Kazmi, A. "The American Muslim Witch Hunt: an inglorious statistic". Cageprisoners. 15 March 2001. www.cageprisoners.com/our-work/blog/item/1326-the-american-muslim-witch-hunt-an-inglorious-statistic.
[136] These organizations, for instance, joined a coalition with Cageprisoners. In August 2011, the coalition decided to boycott a government inquiry into the treatment of detainees. Their joint letter outlining their position, which includes all their logos, can be found at www.reprieve.org.uk/press/2011_08_04_withdrawal_from_inquiry/.
[137] The CCR, Reprieve and Amnesty International supported Begg's 2010 European tour. habibi. "Amnesty UK Tours Begg". *Harry's place.* 11 January 2010. http://hurryupharry.org/2010/01/11/amnesty-uk-tours-begg/.

And yet by examining the available evidence – discounting the FBI confession, which may be tainted, and relying only on open source evidence including Moazzam Begg's memoir, and Cageprisoners' published writings and speeches – we have established the following points:

- Moazzam Begg fought as a foreign jihadi in Bosnia and hoped to do so in Chechnya.

- His bookstore in Birmingham published documents giving lessons on how to conduct jihad, and became a centre for men who wanted to fight in Afghanistan and other places.

- He moved his family to Afghanistan because he supported the Taliban regime.

- He went there to help Abu Rideh, the al-Qaeda recruiter and treasurer, set up a school for the children of foreign jihadis.

- When the US bombed Kabul, he escaped with a group of Pakistani jihadis who took him out via the al-Qaeda escape route at Tora Bora.

- A copy of a bank draft made out to Moazzam Begg was found among abandoned papers at the al-Qaeda training camp at Derunta.

- Since taking over the helm at Cageprisoners, he has become a leading spokesman not only for other imprisoned jihadis, but also for ideas supporting global jihad in general, such as "defensive jihad" and "free the prisoners".

Claudio Cordone, then Interim Secretary-General of Amnesty International, said in an open letter on 28 February 2010: "I wish to stress to you as I have done repeatedly in public that if any evidence emerges that Moazzam Begg or Cageprisoners have promoted views antithetical to human rights, or have been involved in even more sinister activities, Amnesty International would disown its joint advocacy. However, also at play is the old principle that anyone is innocent until proven guilty – not only in a judicial sense."[138]

We trust this study assembles sufficient evidence to demonstrate that Moazzam Begg's views do indeed run counter to principles of universal human rights, and that his actions deserve a closer look than human rights organizations have given them. Some will no doubt continue to maintain all this is nothing more than "guilt by association" or "circumstantial evidence". We would refer them to Henry David Thoreau, who said, in the days when farmers used to water their milk so they would have more to sell, "Some circumstantial evidence is very strong, as when you find a trout in the milk."

Although we disagree profoundly with the worldview of Moazzam Begg and other members of Cageprisoners, we believe that they have every right to their ideas. They also have a right, as do all prisoners of the "war on terror", to due process of law and human rights protections. Our quarrel in this study is less with them than with the human rights organizations that have treated Cageprisoners as a partner and the liberal donors who have considered it a human rights group. What will it take to persuade them to exercise due diligence and look more closely at the politics of those they support?

---

[138] Amnesty International. 2010. "Response to 'The Global Petition to Amnesty International: Restoring the Integrity of Human Rights'". Letter to Amnrita Chhachhi, Sunila Abeysekera and Sara Hossain. Ref. OSG 2010.

If Quaker donors and human rights organizations have been unable to distinguish between human rights and jihadi advocacy groups, it should come as no surprise that the left has had equal or greater problems of discernment.

THE MUSLIM RIGHT AND THE ANGLO-AMERICAN LEFT: THE LOVE THAT DARE NOT SPEAK ITS NAME

As we said in Section I, the Muslim Right is a range of transnational political movements that mobilize identity politics towards the goal of a theocratic state. It consists of those called "moderate Islamists" by the media, who propose to reach this goal gradually by electoral and educational means; extremist parties and groups called "salafis", who run for office but also try to to enforce some version of Sharia law through street violence; and a much smaller militant wing of salafi-jihadis, whose propaganda endorses military means and who practice violence against civilians. The goal of all political Islamists, however, whatever means they may prefer, is a state founded upon a version of Sharia law that systematically discriminates against women along with sexual and religious minorities.

As shown above, some in the human rights movement have gone overboard in their desire to defend the victims of state counter-terrorism, and ended up embracing the Muslim Right. A section of the Anglo-American left has done the same, focusing only on wrongs done by the US and acting on the fatal principle that "the enemy of my enemy is my friend".

Historically, the left has stood for certain values – at least in principle: separation between religion and the state; social equality; an end to discrimination against women and minorities; economic justice; opposition to imperialist and racist wars. In the last ten years, however, some groups on the far left have allied with conservative Muslim organizations that stand for religious discrimination, advocate death for those they consider apostates, oppose gay rights, subordinate women, and seek to impose their views on others through violence. This support of the Muslim Right has undermined struggles for secular democracy in the Global South and has spread from the far left to feminists, the human rights movement and progressive donors.

In 2006, the late Fred Halliday, a socialist public intellectual and expert on the Middle East, listed some ways that left wing movements were giving support to the Muslim Right.[139]   He included the Tehran visit of Venezuelan socialist leader Hugo Chavez, during which Chavez embraced Iranian president Ahmadinejad;[140] the official welcome ceremony given by Ken Livingston, then Mayor of London, and MP George Galloway of the Respect Party, to Yusuf al-Qaradawi, a controversial Egyptian cleric associated with the Muslim Brotherhood; and the alignment of the Socialist Workers Party with Islamists in the Stop the War movement, in which London antiwar demonstrators carried signs saying, "We are all Hezbollah". He might also have included the fact that the Third European Social Forum, meeting in London in 2004, prominently featured Tariq Ramadan, a professor of Contemporary Islamic Studies at Oxford University, while denying a feminist coalition

---

[139] Halliday, F. 2007. "The Jihadism of Fools", *Dissent*, Winter. www.dissentmagazine.org/article/the-jihadism-of-fools. A shorter version of the article was published by *openDemocracy.net* on 7 September 2006 under the title "The Left and Jihadis".

[140] Their mutual oil interest was certainly a factor here, and Chavez has also embraced other authoritarian leaders, such as Alexander Lukashenko of Belarus, who is known as the last Stalinist dictator in Europe.

space for a panel on "Unholy Alliances" between the left and the Muslim Right.[141]

A particularly egregious example of this trend is left wing support for "the Iraqi insurgency",[142] which includes groups allied with al-Qaeda and is made up of Sunni militants who practice sectarian violence against Shi'a and plant bombs in marketplaces and civilian neighbourhoods. Although Iraqi leftists and feminists oppose the Iraqi insurgency, some antiwar coalitions in the North have endorsed it on the basis that it is fighting foreign invasion and imperialism.[143] In fact, the insurgency has directed its violence less at the US than at imposing an Islamic state on its own people, targeting women in particular, as Anissa Hélie, a feminist scholar and former coordinator of Women Living Under Muslim Laws, pointed out in 2005:

---

[141] The coalition included Women Living Under Muslim Laws, Women Against Fundamentalism, Women in Black, Catholics for a Free Choice and Act Together (an Iraqi-British solidarity group).
[142] At a 2004 antiwar conference in Japan, some groups advocated supporting the Islamist insurgency on the grounds that it was effective against the US; others argued that the insurgency was composed of Islamists who oppress other Iraqis. Those in favour of supporting the insurgency were primarily Trotskyist groups: the US coalition A.N.S.W.E.R. (Act Now to End War and Stop Racism), which is dominated by the International Action Center and Workers World Party, and the Stop the War Coalition in the UK, which is dominated by the Socialist Workers Party. Kazuyoshi, S. Not dated. "Significance of Building Solidarity with Iraqi Civic Resistance". http://www.mdsweb. jp/international/magazine/r56/i_r56t2.html. For a call by Sharon Smith of the SWP to support the Iraqi insurgency see, "The Antiwar Movement and the Iraqi Resistance". *Counterpunch*, 21-23 January 2005. http://www.counterpunch.org/smith01212005.html.
[143] Both the A.N.S.W.E.R. Coalition in the US and the Stop the War Coalition in the UK have explicitly supported Sunni sectarian terrorism.

For example, an extremist group in Iraq called Mujahideen Shura (council of fighters) warned it would kill any woman who is seen unveiled on the street. The recent case of Zeena Al Qushtaini has shown this is not an empty threat. Zeena, a women's rights activist and businesswoman known for wearing "Western" clothing, was kidnapped and executed by Jamaat al Tawhid wa'l-Jihad, another armed Islamist group. Her body was found wrapped in the traditional abaya, which she had refused to wear when she was alive. Pinned to the abaya was the message: "She was a collaborator against Islam". Muslim extremists have already moved on to assassinating male and female hairdressers whom they accuse of promoting "Western" fashion. They also specifically target trade union leaders as well as gays and lesbians. Religious minorities are also under attack, such as Christians in the Northern city of Mosul where women from the Christian community were singled out in a rape campaign.[144]

Despite this record, prominent left wing intellectuals in the UK like Tariq Ali, an editor of *New Left Review*, continued to romanticize Iraqi sectarian attacks: "There is also the political resistance of Moqtada al-Sadr and his faction, which is based in the Sh'ia slums of Baghdad and the poor sectors of Basra and other cities in the south of Iraq. He will demand the withdrawal of all foreign troops and say no to permanent US bases in the

---

[144] "The US Occupation and Rising Religious Extremism: The Double Threat to Women in Iraq", *Different Takes, A Publication of the Population and Development Program at Hampshire College*, No. 35, Summer 2005. See also Worth, R. F. 2005. "A haircut in Iraq can be the death of the barber", *The New York Times*, 18 March; Osborn, M. 2005. "Iraqi Union leader murdered. 'Resistance' targets trade unions, women, lesbians and gay men", *Workers' Liberty*, 12 January.

country."[145] Though Ali wrote this in 2005, when the events Hélie notes were already on record, he said not a word about the attacks of this "resistance" upon Iraqi civilians.

Another aspect of the far left's embrace of Islamic fundamentalism is the way it mirrors distortions about Islam put about by anti-immigrant conservatives – the far right talks as if all Muslims were potential terrorists, while the far left talks as if salafi-jihadis represented all Muslims. Both ignore the fact that the vast majority of Muslims are like everybody else; they just want to survive and live their lives in peace. Very few of them support the interpretations and actions of salafi-jihadis,[146] who no more represent all Muslims than the American Nazi Party or English Defence League represent all Christians.

Ironically, some states, including the UK, have adopted the same approach; in the name of multiculturalism, they have taken organizations led by Muslim extremists to represent the population as a whole, not only recognizing but also funding identity-based groups associated with the Muslim Brotherhood and Jamaat e Islaami.[147] Canada has taken a similar approach, as noted

---

[145] "Tariq Ali on empire and those who fight it", *Socialist Worker*, 19 March 2005.
[146] Pew Global Attitudes Project. "Islamic Extremism: Common Concern for Muslim and Western Publics". Pew Research Center. 14 July 2005. http://www.pewglobal.org/2005/07/14/islamic-extremism-common-concern-for-muslim-and-western-publics/. A *Daily Telegraph* survey in 2005 showed that only 6 per cent of British Muslims approved of the 7 July 2005 bombings, though far more sympathized with the motives of the attackers. King, A. 2005. "One in four Muslims sympathizes with motives of terrorists", *Daily Telegraph*, 23 July.
[147] See, for instance, Townsend, M. and H. Olivennes. 2011. "PM wins row with Nick Clegg over crackdown on Muslim extremists", *The Guardian*, 4 June; "Updated anti-extremism strategy published", *BBC News*, 7 June 2011.

by sociologist Haideh Moghissi, a professor at Toronto's York University:

> Western governments and the media seem determined to promote the punishing, unforgiving and violent voices of Islam. Worse, taking them as the authentic and representative voices of Muslims worldwide, they are made legitimate partners at negotiation tables whenever there is a need to address the interests and grievances of Muslim populations. By making religion the guiding principle in their foreign policy and in dealing with their own ethnic minorities, these governments follow, in a sense, the agenda of conservative Muslims, rather than stressing and protecting the hard-won secular political values and practices of their societies. From my perspective, it is hard not to worry about some ill-advised government policies, such as allowing Friday prayers in publicly funded middle schools in Toronto, which includes hiring an imam to lead the prayers for thirteen- and fourteen-year-old students.[148]

With similar political blindness, sections of the international left have continued to support the Iranian theocracy despite its violent repression of the "Green Revolution" of 2009-2010, its attacks on student and women's organizations, and its suppression of labour unions. In September 2010, for instance, 150 self-described "progressive activists" in the US, led by former US Attorney General Ramsey Clark and former member of the House of Representatives Cynthia McKinney, dined with Iranian President Ahmadinejad on his visit to the UN to show their support for his allegedly anti-imperialist stand.

---

[148] Moghissi, H. "What We Have Learned from 9/11". *10 Years After September 11: A Social Science Research Council Essay Forum.* 8 September 2011. http://essays.ssrc.org/10yearsafter911/what-we-have-learned-from-911/.

Left wing supporters of Ahmadinejad are willing to overlook the fact that he is not only a dictator and fundamentalist but also a Holocaust denier; they also make other concessions to anti-Semitism.[149] By this we do not mean legitimate criticism of Israeli violations of Palestinian human rights, but the use of ancient racist stereotypes about Jewish bankers and "Zionist-Hindu-Crusader-Masonic" alliances that secretly control the world – the kind of stereotyping that would rightly be rejected in an eruption of political correctness if applied to Muslims or blacks. Some on the left have even bought into the "truther" belief, endorsed by Ahmadinejad, that either the US government or Mossad planned the 9/11 attack – a notion angrily rebutted by al-Qaeda spokesman Ayman al-Zawahiri, who accused Iran and Hezbollah of spreading this rumor in order to detract from al-Qaeda's achievements.[150]

Unwillingness to criticize the Iranian theocracy has led to a lack of solidarity with the people of Iran, a particular problem at a time of sanctions and talk of war. In March 2012, a United National Antiwar Coalition met in Hartford to oppose the possibility of war with Iran, condemn sanctions, and oppose US wars and interference in other places.[151] By an overwhelming majority,

---

[149] For more on this see, Alan, A. "Why Things Are This Bad". *Harry's place*. 25 April 2012. http://hurryupharry.org/2012/04/25/why-things-are-this-bad/; Cohen, N. 2012. "How the Left Turned Against the Jews", *Standpoint*, April.
[150] "Al-Qaeda accuses Iran of 9/11 lie", *BBC News*, 22 April 2008.
[151] United Antiwar Coalition. Not dated. "Who We Are". https://nationalpeaceconference.org/Purpose_of_Conference.html. The conference was called by the following organizations, among others: Muslim Peace Coalition, Veterans for Peace, International Action Center, Black Agenda Report, May 1 Immigrant and Workers Rights Coalition, Fellowship of Reconciliation, Center for Constitutional Rights, Voices for Creative Nonviolence, Desis Rising Up and Moving (DRUM), Women's International League for Peace and Freedom (WILPF), Code Pink Maine, and International Socialist Organization (ISO).

---

however, the meeting refused to support the human rights of the Iranian people, voting down a resolution that said, "We oppose war and sanctions against the Iranian people and stand in solidarity with their struggle against state repression and all forms of outside intervention."[152]

And yet, as a spokeswoman for the New York-based Raha Iranian Feminists Group, which supported the defeated resolution, said,

> If we don't support Iranians struggling in Iran for the same things we fight for here, such as labour rights, abolition of the death penalty and freedom for political prisoners, we risk a politically debilitating form of cultural relativism. At best we are hypocrites; at worst we show an inability to imagine Iranians as anything other than passive victims of Western powers. Ironically, this echoes racist and Orientalist stereotypes of the kind that most antiwar activists would hasten to decry.[153]

The antiwar movement's courtship of the Muslim Right went even further in the UK, where, in 2001, the Socialist Workers Party initiated the Stop the War Coalition, which two years later organized the largest UK antiwar demonstration ever, against the war in Iraq. They did so in partnership with the Campaign for Nuclear Disarmament and the Muslim Association of Britain,

---

[152] Nasrabadi, M. 2012. "Iran and the U.S. Antiwar Movement", *Jadaliyya*, 8 May.
[153] *Ibid.*
[154] See Rayner, G. 2006. "Terror link of 'moderate' Muslims at London rally", *Daily Mail*, 11 February; Vidino, L. "Current Trends and Methods of Europe's Muslim Brotherhood". Hudson Institute, Center on Islam, Democracy, and the Future of the Muslim World. 1 November 2006. http://currenttrends.org/research/detail/aims-and-methods-of-europes-muslim-brotherhood; AWAAZ-South Asia Watch, op. cit.

which is associated with the Muslim Brotherhood.[154] The SWP was carrying out a policy outlined by Chris Harman, one of its leaders. As early as 1994, Harman wrote that the left must not regard Islamists as the enemy because "they are not responsible for the system of international capitalism." Rather, their "feeling of revolt" should be "tapped for progressive purposes",[155] meaning that the SWP should try to manipulate the Muslim Right into supporting left wing objectives. In pursuit of this plan, the SWP made remarkable concessions for a Marxist organization that theoretically stands for equality between men and women, going as far as allowing gender-segregated seating (reportedly for Asian women only) at antiwar meetings. When questioned on this, the secretary of the Stop the War Coalition described women's rights and gay rights as a "shibboleth", an outmoded belief that could not be allowed to get in the way of unity with Muslim groups.[156]

The alliance with the Stop the War Coalition brought new strength and visibility to the Muslim Brotherhood's organization in the UK. According to one analyst, because of this campaign the Muslim Association of Britain grew "from a relatively obscure group to one with a national profile. It gained considerable influence, punching well above the weight suggested by its limited membership and narrow formal constituency ... Its membership rose from 400 to 800 or 1,000 – still small, of course, but twice its original size."[157] While English Trotskyites were elated by the success of this alliance, an Iraqi leftist who attended a 2003 conference of the Stop the War Coalition came

---

[155] Bassi, C. Not dated. "'The Anti-Imperialism of Fools': A Cautionary Story on the Revolutionary Socialist Vanguard of England's Post-9/11 Anti-War Movement". *Acme*. www.acme-journal.org/vol9/Bassi10.pdf.
[156] Day, A. 2004. "Hammer and Crescent", *New Humanist*, Volume 119 Issue 1, January/February.
[157] Phillips, R. 2008. "Standing Together: the Muslim Association of Britain and the anti-war movement", *Race and Class*, 50:101.

away in despair at the folly of the SWP in building up the Muslim Right, saying, "Ironically, political Islam is applauded and welcomed by the SWP, while both ordinary Muslims in the Middle East and in Western society, and Western people reject it."[158]

Beyond opportunism and the desire to have big demonstrations, what accounts for this folly? Left wing support for the Muslim Right proceeds from five wrong ideas about world politics.

---

[158] Mohammed, S. 2003. "The SWP and political Islam: lending support to anti-worker movement", *Workers Liberty* 3/23, 6 February.

FIVE WRONG IDEAS ABOUT THE MUSLIM RIGHT

WRONG IDEA 1: THE MUSLIM RIGHT IS ANTI-IMPERIALIST

Some on the far left support the Taliban, the Iraqi insurgency, the Iranian theocracy and even al-Qaeda, in the belief that they systematically oppose US imperialism. This idea does not accord with reality:

— The Taliban began as an ally of the US, financed by the CIA, Pakistan and Saudi Arabia to fight the Soviets in Afghanistan.

— Most of the people killed by salafi-jihadis in Afghanistan, Iraq, Nigeria, Yemen, and everywhere else they are fighting are not US soldiers but other Muslims, or local people of various religions. A 2009 study of Arabic media sources by the Combating Terrorism Centre at West Point, in New York State, found that only 15 per cent of all of the casualties caused by al-Qaeda between 2004 and 2008 were Westerners. Between 2006 and 2008, the most recent period the study examined, fully 98 per cent of al-Qaeda's victims were inhabitants of Muslim majority countries.[159]

---

[159] Al-Obaidi, M, N. Abdullah, S. Helfstein. *Deadly Vanguards: A Study of al-Qa'ida's Violence Against Muslims*. Combating Terrorism Center at West Point. 1 December 2009. Downloadable pdf at www.ctc.usma.edu/posts/deadly-vanguards-a-study-of-al-qaidas-violence-against-muslims.

━━ The main financial support for salafi-jihadi groups comes from various sources in Saudi Arabia, arguably the most reactionary country in the world and a staunch ally of the same US imperialists that jihadis say they are fighting.

Even if the Muslim Right were a reliable foe of US imperialism, "The enemy of my enemy is my friend" is a very poor strategy for left wing survival. Wherever Islamists have gained power, they have wiped out the left – see Algeria, Indonesia, Iran, Sudan, and, of course, Afghanistan.[160] Women Living Under Muslim Laws, an international network with over 25 years experience documenting Muslim politico-religious forces, made this point in a 2005 appeal to the World Social Forum in Porto Alegre:

> Fundamentalist terror is by no means a tool of the poor against the rich, of the Third World against the West, of people against capitalism. It is not a legitimate response that can be supported by the progressive forces of the world. Its main target is the internal democratic opposition to [its] theocratic project ... of controlling all aspects of society in the name of religion, including education, the legal system, youth services, etc. When fundamentalists come to power, they silence the people; they physically eliminate dissidents, writers, journalists, poets, musicians, painters like fascists do. Like fascists, they physically eliminate the "untermensch" – the subhuman – among them "inferior races", gays, mentally or physically disabled people. And they lock women "in their place", which as we know from experience ends up being a strait jacket. Like fascists, they support capitalism.[161]

---

160 Halliday, *Dissent*, op.cit.
161 "WLUML Statement to the World Social Forum – Appeal Against Fundamentalisms". Women Living Under Muslim Laws. 21 January 2005. http://www.wluml.org/node/1850.

A variant of the "enemy of my enemy" theory invokes a crude version of Marxism to explain that, since US imperialism is the principal enemy of the world's people, we should defeat it before worrying about other enemies. According to Vijay Prashad, a professor at Trinity College and author of *The Darker Nations: A History of the Third World:*

> In today's world, the principal contradiction, the Large Contradiction, is between imperialism and humanity ... The Lesser Contradiction is between the left and the reactionaries, who are not identical to imperialism. Indian Hindutva, American evangelicalism and Zionism are reactionary, but not part of the Lesser Contradiction. Those forms of reaction are ensconced in the Larger Contradiction, since they are handmaidens of imperialism. What I refer to as the reactionaries of the Lesser Contradiction are organizations such as Hezbollah and Hamas, the Muslim Brotherhood and so on ... These other groups are antagonistic to imperialism, and are from this standpoint able to capture the sentiments and politics of the people who are anti-imperialist nationalists. We are divided from them, but not against them in the same way as we are against imperialism. To make these two contradictions the same is to fall into the liberal error of equivalence.[162]

One of the problems with this approach is that while the left is battling the Large Contradiction the Lesser Contradiction is likely to sneak up on it, as WLUML demonstrates, citing an Erich Fried poem to this effect:

---

[162] "'It prefigures for the Arab people a new horizon': Vijay Prashad on the Arab revolt (Part II)". *Radical Notes.* 1 February 2011. http://radicalnotes.com/tag/vijay-prashad/.

Totally caught into my struggle against the main enemy
I was shot by my secondary enemy.
Not from the back, treacherously, as his main enemies
claimed
But directly, from the position he had long been
occupying
And in keeping with his declared intentions that I did
not bother about,
thinking they were insignificant.[163]

Besides, shouldn't anti-imperialism mean opposition to all forms of imperialism? Salafi-jihadis speak of establishing a new Caliphate or pan-Islamic empire, in which only practicing Muslims would be full citizens and non-believers would either be wiped out or live as second-class subjects.[164] How can any group that is trying to establish an empire of its own be called anti-imperialist?

WRONG IDEA 2: "DEFENCE OF MUSLIM LANDS" IS COMPARABLE TO NATIONAL LIBERATION STRUGGLES

In his *Defence of Muslim Lands*, the 1979 fatwa calling foreign fighters to Afghanistan, Abdullah Azzam developed the idea that it is legitimate in international law for foreign fighters to

---

[163] Fried, E. 1978. *Cent poèmes sans frontière*. Cited in WLUML, Dossier 30-31, "The struggle for secularism in Europe and North America". Downloadable at www.wluml.org/resource/dossier-30-31-struggle-secularism-europe-and-north-america.
[164] Hizb ut-Tahrir and the Muslim Brotherhood wish to do this by parliamentary means while al-Qaeda favours the use of force.

make war anywhere in the world in "self-defence" of "Muslim lands" and that this is comparable to the right of national self-determination. Other salafi-jihadi spokespeople and some on the left echo this claim.

Those who invoke "defensive jihad" usually refer to a list of conflict zones – including Afghanistan, Bosnia, Chechnya, Iraq, Kashmir and Palestine – that are to be liberated from foreigners (or from the wrong kind of Muslim, depending on the audience being addressed). Such "Muslim lands" must be returned to the control of "proper thinking" (i.e. fundamentalist) believers. Some salafi groups advocate doing this by peaceful means, others by jihad, but all aim at an Islamic empire under some version of Sharia law.[165]

Salafi-jihadi spokesmen continually compare the "defence of Muslim lands" to the national liberation struggles of the 1960s and 70s, particularly that of South Africa. Their mantra is, "Today's terrorist is tomorrow's freedom fighter". But the aims of yesterday's national liberation movements had almost nothing in common with those of today's jihadis. Not only were these national liberation struggles trying to establish modern, independent nation-states, free of colonial domination, many of them, at least in theory, also had explicit goals of economic and social equality for all. They were not aiming for a pan-national empire ruled by a hierarchical religious authority, offering forced conversion, unequal citizenship, or death to "infidels".

---

[165] As Women Living Under Muslim Laws has demonstrated over three decades, what people actually mean by Sharia varies widely from one place to another, but Islamist groups all think their own interpretation is the only legitimate one. See also note 27.

The hollowness of the comparison to national liberation struggles can currently be seen in the north of Mali, where the form of Sufi Islam practiced by the local population is considered "kuffar" by salafi-jihadists allied to al-Qaeda. In April 2011 the Movement for the National Liberation of Azawad (MNLA) took over the region and proclaimed it a Taureg republic. Almost immediately, the MNLA was displaced by three aggressive Islamist groups, Ansar Dine, al-Qaeda in the Islamic Magreb (AQIM) and Movement for Oneness and Jihad in West Africa (MUJAO). Far from declaring national liberation, Ansar Dine announced, "We are against independence. We are against revolutions [that are] not in the name of Islam."[166] The aim is to impose their version of Muslim law upon the native population – blocking TV signals, banning alcohol and music, insisting that women veil, cutting off hands for robbery, stoning couples to death who had children without being married and destroying the ancient monuments of Timbuktu. This has nothing to do with self-determination by local Malians, who are fleeing the area in massive numbers.[167]

Why then is this comparison with national liberation struggles so frequently made? Partly to attract support from the left and partly to drape "defence of Muslim lands" in the mantle of a human rights struggle, since the right to national self-determination is recognized in the Universal Declaration of Human Rights. But it is obvious that the goal of a pan-Islamic state ruled by a version of Sharia law directly contravenes most of the articles in the Declaration including Article 7 ("All are equal

---

[166] Cafiero, G. "Understanding the Standoff in Mali". *Foreign Policy in Focus.* 3 August 2012. www.fpif.org/articles/understanding_the_standoff_in_mali.
[167] Nossiter, A. 2012. "Islamists in North Mali Amputate Man's Hand", *The New York Times*, 9 August and "Islamists in North Mali Stone Couple to Death", 30 July.

before the law"), Article 18 ("Everyone has the right to freedom of thought, conscience and religion") and the provisions for women's equality. There is no basis in theory or practice that would allow a human rights organization to endorse "defensive jihad" without betraying its own principles.[168]

And what are these "Muslim lands" invoked by comparisons to national liberation struggles? Are they the lands controlled by Turkey during the widest extent of the Ottoman Empire, which would include most of the Middle East, North Africa, the Caucasus Emirate and large parts of Eastern Europe? What about Pakistan, India, Indonesia, Malaysia, the Philippines? What about Mali, Niger, Nigeria, Senegal, Somalia? What about Western countries with substantial Muslim populations? Not all salafi-jihadis have the same definition of the territory they plan to liberate. The Indonesian group Jemaah Islamiya, for instance, has in mind an Asian version of the Caliphate stretching from southern Thailand through Malaysia across Indonesia and into the Philippines, which would link with other branches established by al-Qaeda.[169]

In fact, the category "Muslim lands", like the similar category "the Muslim world", is not historical but political; the term became prominent only after the rise of the identity politics of the 1990s. As Sami Zubaida, professor emeritus of politics and sociology at Birkbeck College, University of London, explains:

> "Umma nationalism" [is] the idea that Muslims in the world are a unitary community under attack from hostile

---

[168] Despite this fact, Amnesty International endorsed "defensive jihad" in its 2010 disagreement with Gita Sahgal; see, Tax, op. cit.
[169] Pavlova, E. 2006. "From Counter-Society to Counter-State: Jemaah Islamiyah According to Pupji". Institute of Defence and Strategic Studies. Downloadable pdf at www.rsis.edu.sg/publications/ WorkingPapers/WP120.pdf, p. 11.

forces also identified as Christians ("Crusaders"), Jews and Hindus ... Part of this Umma nationalism is to view certain wars or conflicts as attacks on Muslims as a whole, such as those occurring in Afghanistan, Pakistan, Palestine and Iraq. This conception obscures the imperialist and geo-political nature of these conflicts, and the fact that almost all of them involve conflicts in which Muslims fight on opposite sides. In Afghanistan, Pakistan and Iraq, it is primarily Muslims who have killed large numbers of other Muslims over the past years. Sectarian and doctrinal identities are superimposed on conflicts over power, territory and resources. Muslim rulers and dynasties, notably the impeccably Islamic Saudis, are intimate allies of the US. To label all these conflicts and wars as attacks on Muslims is not only wrong but also politically counter-productive, for it obscures the real issues at stake.[170]

WRONG IDEA 3: THE PROBLEM IS "ISLAMOPHOBIA"

To understand this issue, we must unpack the concept of "Islamophobia",[171] which includes two main and very different meanings. In popular speech and the media, the term is used to mean discrimination, prejudice, hatred of, and violent attacks

---

[170] Zubaida, S. 2012. "The Diversity of Muslims and the Necessity of Secular Rule", in N. Yuval-Davis and P. Marfleet (eds), *Secularism, Racism and the Politics of Belonging. Runnymede Perspectives*, pp. 33-34. Downloadable pdf at www.runnymedetrust.org/.../pdfs/...

[171] UK sources attribute popularization of the term to a 1997 publication by the anti-racist Runnymede Trust, while French sources attribute it to Ayatollah Khomeini, who said Iranian women who rejected the veil were "Islamophobic". Javeau, C. 2009. Preface, in N. Geerts, *Fichu Voile! Petit argumentaire laique, feministe et antiraciste*, L. Pire (ed.), Paris, p.11.

upon Muslims in the West. Blanket police surveillance is sometimes included in this usage. When used by Islamists, the term includes any criticism of their ideas and practices, or Muslim texts. It also includes invasions of "Muslim lands," which are attributed to a hatred of Islam rather than to geopolitical reasons like the desire to control territory, trade or oil.

In popular speech: Hatred of and discrimination against Muslims

There can be no question that right wing forces in Europe, the US and the UK have organized anti-Muslim campaigns and sought to mobilize prejudice for political ends. This was evident in electioneering by politicians like Sarkozy and Le Pen in France, popular campaigns by English fascists, and a number of demagogic efforts in the US such as the campaigns against the so-called "Ground Zero Mosque" and Debbie Almontaser, founding principal of the Khalil Gibran Academy in New York, not to mention the Koran-burning publicity stunts by Pastor Terry Jones in Florida.[172] While

---

[172] Nicholas Sarkozy was president of France, 2007-2012. He attempted to win re-election in the 2012 presidential election by appealing to anti-immigration sentiments. Marine Le Pen is a French politician of the far right National Front who ran for parliament in 2012 on an anti-immigration, anti-Muslim platform. The so-called "Ground Zero Mosque", also called "Park 51", is a Muslim community centre planned for lower Manhattan, which became the object of a right wing campaign in 2010, when conservatives called it a deliberate attempt to desecrate the site of the former World Trade Center – it was actually located some distance away. In 2007, Debbie Almontaser, the founder of the Khalil Gibran International Academy, an Arabic-themed dual language school in Brooklyn, was forced to resign before the school could open after a campaign by the *New York Post* attempted to brand her as a dangerous Muslim radical. See Elliot, A. 2008. "Critics Cost Muslim Educator Her Dream School", *The New York Times*, 28 April.

---

these campaigns were designed to whip up fear of "the other", there was nothing irrational or "phobic" about them; they were calculated acts of anti-Muslim demagogy. Such campaigns should be exposed and fought using the usual methods of fighting racial and religious discrimination.

Nor is there anything irrational about US policies of police over-reach, targeting and entrapment.[173] The time-honored methods of wiretapping, infiltration, and provocation now being used against Muslims were used against the Civil Rights movement and New Left in the sixties and against the Communist Party and labour movement earlier. These are ways of beefing up the police force (with Homeland Security money) and further militarizing social control.

Police interventions and rightwing campaigns aside, however, most anti-Muslim prejudice in Europe and the US can be attributed to classic racism and fear of "the other". In the US, similar anti-immigrant campaigns have been organized in years past against Irish immigrants, Eastern European Jews, Chinese, Mexicans, and Central Americans. Racial and ethnic stereotypes invoking fears of invasion by an alien people with a high birthrate and different language, religion, or customs have been mobilized against each of these populations in turn. And such racial stereotypes and fears have been used against African-Americans and American Indians from the beginning.

---

[173] See, for instance, Bayoumi, M. 2011. "Peter King's 'Islamic Radicalism' Hearings Fan Paranoid Fantasies", *The Nation*, 10 March;Shachtman, N. and S. Ackerman. 2012. "U.S. Military Taught Officers: Use 'Hiroshima Tactics' for 'Total War' on Islam". *Wired*, 10 May; Blumenthal, M. 2010. "The Great Fear". *TomDispatch*. 19 December 2010. www.tomdispatch.com/post/175334/tomgram:_max_blumenthal,_the_great_fear/.

Certainly South Asian and Arab-Americans in the US experienced an elevated level of threat and insecurity after 9/11 – in one case, a Sikh was killed by nativist thugs who thought he was a Muslim – and both mosques and Sikh temples are still subject to arson and attacks by white racist terrorists. Mosques have also been subject to intense police surveillance. But to characterize such events as the result of a phobia, or irrational hatred, is to de-politicize them. Racism does have its pathological and phobic aspects and, in some festering corners of the American psyche, anti-Muslim antipathy was no doubt fed by the election of a dark-skinned President with an African father and the middle name Hussain. Nevertheless, the problem of racism has to be approached politically.

Like the US, European countries have been struggling with "the other", but have been historically more homogeneous and less welcoming of immigrants than the US, and more open to fascism. As Gary Younge recounted in 2010:

> In the Netherlands in June the party of Geert Wilders, who calls Muslims 'goat fuckers' and wants to ban the Koran, almost tripled its representation, becoming the third-largest party. In 'liberal' Sweden in September the hard-right Sweden Democrats entered parliament for the first time, with 5.7 per cent of the vote. With extremist parties regularly getting more than 10 per cent, and in some cases sitting in government, European fascism has returned as a mainstream ideology. These movements start off on the fringes, but like arsenic in the water supply, their policies and rhetoric have a tendency to infect the broader discourse.[174]

---

[174] "Islamophobia – European Style", *The Nation*, 23 September 2010.

While fascist groups and nativist politicians do their best to whip up prejudice against immigrants, and are currently focusing on Muslims for that purpose, is discrimination against Muslims actually worse than, say, racism against people of Caribbean descent in the UK or Latino/as and African-Americans in the US? If police harassment is a criterion, most Muslims in the UK are South Asian but, in 2002-2003, young Caribbean men were five times more likely to be stopped and frisked by the police than their South Asian counterparts.[175] If being stopped and asked to show your papers, or being arrested for small amounts of marijuana are criteria, the main targets in the US are Latino/a immigrants and African-Americans. On the other hand, surveillance of shops and religious institutions is targeted mostly at Muslims.

In the US, the FBI's 2010 survey of hate crimes showed that "47.3 per cent were motivated by a racial bias, 20 per cent were motivated by a religious bias, 19.3 per cent were motivated by a sexual orientation bias and 12.8 per cent were motivated by an ethnicity/national origin bias."[176] Of hate crimes motivated by

---

[175] Malik, K. 2009. *From Fatwa to Jihad: The Rushdie Affair and its Legacy*. London: Atlantic Books, p. 135. According to the Center for Constitutional Rights, in New York City in 2011, "685,724 people were stopped, 84 per cent of whom were Black and Latino residents – although they comprise only about 23 per cent and 29 per cent of New York City's total population respectively." "Stop and Frisk – The Human Impact: The Stories Behind the Numbers, the Effects on our Communities". 2012. http://ccrjustice.org/stopandfrisk. In France, the numbers are closer. According to a report by Human Rights Watch, "A 2009 study by the Open Society Justice Initiative and the French National Center for Scientific Research found that in France, black people were six times as likely as white people, and Arabs almost eight times as likely, to be stopped." "France: Abusive Checks of Minority Youth". Human Rights Watch. 26 January 2012. www.hrw.org/news/2012/01/26/france-abusive-identity-checks-minority-youth.

religion in 2010, 65.4 per cent were anti-Jewish, 13.2 per cent were anti-Muslim, and the rest were spread out over everybody else. But all the anti-religious hate crimes put together were significantly fewer than racist hate crimes against African-Americans.[177] And that's not even counting bias crimes by the police. In short, the picture is complicated, and while persecution of Muslims must be fought, it should not blind us to continuing institutionalized racism against other groups.

In Islamist speech: Attacks on sacred texts or on "Muslim lands"

When Islamists use the term "Islamophobia" they fold other concepts into the popular usage above. For instance, because they do not admit the legitimacy of any criticism of sacred texts, they describe anyone who criticizes Muslim laws on women as "Islamophobic". The purpose is to cut off criticism. But Muslim laws are historic documents, which can no more be protected from critical examination than the sacred texts of other religions; both the Torah and the New Testament have plenty of retrograde pronouncements on women, and it is anyone's right to point these out.

In fact, Islamist usage of the term "Islamophobia" is a major reason to avoid using the word when describing discriminatory acts or hate speech. Anti-Muslim actions or speech are directed at individuals or institutions and they have remedies in the law. But what is the remedy for "Islamophobia", when framed as prejudice against

---

[176] "FBI Releases 2010 Hate Crime Statistics". FBI. 14 November 2011. www.fbi.gov/news/pressrel/press-releases-2010-hate-crime-statistics/.
[177] *Ibid.*

sacred texts or a whole religion? The remedy usually recommended is censorship – a violation of basic human rights – or laws against blasphemy, which amount to the same thing. And what about disagreements among Muslims, and Muslims who dissent from fundamentalist interpretations? Who will protect their right to dissent if any such disagreement is conflated with hate speech? Rather than focusing on discrimination against individuals on account of their religion, the word "Islamophobia" focuses on protecting the religion itself, and the effect is to promote censorship.

Another meaning of "Islamophobia" when used by Islamists is the belief that wars being conducted in "Muslim lands" are happening because the people who live there are Muslims – i.e., that these are wars of religion rather than wars for geopolitical reasons. The countries invoked for purposes of this argument are usually Bosnia, Iraq, Afghanistan and Palestine.

This idea may hold up in the case of Bosnia, where Serbia's mobilization of ethnic hatred resulted in genocidal attacks on Muslims. Though the mobilization of anti-Muslim hatred was not the only factor in the Yugoslav war – which also included war between Orthodox Serbs and Catholic Croats – it was an important aspect of Serbian ultra-nationalism. But is difficult to argue that the wars in Afghanistan and Iraq are religious in origin or nature. Most of the people fighting on both sides are Muslims. If the Bush Administration was keen to invade Iraq because of its oil, the main rationale for the war in Afghanistan was the fact that the Taliban gave a safe haven to Osama bin Laden. And while the conflict between Israel and Palestine has a religious aspect, and is exacerbated by the rise of fundamentalism on both sides, territorial and political arguments stemming from the occupation are far more prominent.

Some on the left, however, have adopted the Muslim Right's usage of "Islamophobia", as in a speech by Michael Ratner, President of the Center for Constitutional Rights, at a Cageprisoners meeting in January 2012: "I am convinced that Gitmo and other places like Gitmo only exist because its detainees are Muslims. I can't imagine a Christian Gitmo. I cannot imagine a Jewish Guantanamo. It exists because of Islamophobia."[178]

An uncritical adoption of the concept of Islamophobia leads to such grand ahistorical claims. For this reason we believe that, while it is essential that the progressive movement fight racism and prejudice against Muslims, the term "Islamophobia" tends to echo the framing of the Muslim Right, which can lead to efforts to criminalize free expression and dissent; it thus does more to confuse the issues than clarify them.

WRONG IDEA 4: TERRORISM IS JUSTIFIED BY REVOLUTIONARY NECESSITY

Since the French and Bolshevik Revolutions, if not before, the left has had a tendency to see terrorism either as a legitimate expression of popular grievances or as necessary to protect the gains of the revolution. The communist left was understanding about Stalin's terror, and parts of the New Left were willing to excuse China's Cultural Revolution and terror by the Khmer Rouge, Sendero Luminoso, the Tamil Tigers, and the Columbian FARQ. Today some on the left are equally forgiving of terror by the Muslim Right, seeing it as insignificant compared to wars and drone killings. Take,

---

[178] CP Editor. "Michael Ratner, President of the Center for Constitutional Rights at Cageprisoners: How did Guantanamo get there"? 28 June 2012. www.cageprisoners.com/our-work/interviews/item/4509-michael-ratner-%E2%80%9Chow-did-gitmo-get-there?-only-exists-because-detainees-are-muslims%E2%80%9D.

for instance, this response by Corinna Mullin, a lecturer at the School of Oriental and African Studies, to Anissa Hélie's critique of leftist support for the Islamist insurgency in Iraq, already quoted above:

> It is unclear if Hélie's problem lies with armed resistance, in general, or specifically, with armed resistance carried out by people who hold different beliefs to her own. She is certainly right that there "are plenty of unarmed civilians, as well as groups of every political affiliation, that reject the US occupation yet do not engage in violence or human rights violations", as there were in the Algerian independence war, which she references. But as Hélie may also recall, the issue of indiscriminate attacks, or "terrorism", was also criticized by many on the European left during that time who, like Hélie, were also weary of the "by any means necessary" argument, perhaps because they didn't understand the nature of asymmetric warfare and/or had little experience with the type of desperation that is born out of the exploitative and brutal conditions engendered by colonialism/occupation ... Granted, the sectarian violence is somewhat different in nature, but still it is an issue that must be seen, like "terrorism", within the context of colonialism/neo-colonialism and occupation.[179]

Such left wing defences of terrorism have three ideological roots: the belief that terror is an attack upon the power of the

---

[179] Mullin, C. "Reply to Anissa Hélie's 'The U.S. Occupation and Rising Religious Extremism: the Double Threat to Women in Iraq'". *Znet*. 12 July 2005. www.zcommunications.org/reply-to-anissa-helies-the-u-s-occupation-and-rising-religious-extremism-the-double-threat-to-women-in-iraq-by-corinna-mullin.

state, when it is usually an attack upon civilians; the belief that the end justifies the means; and the belief that only violence can defeat violence.

Most terrorist actions are not directed at the state. Even large-scale attacks on civilians like the 7/7 bombing of underground trains and buses in London and the 9/11 air attack on the World Trade Center and Pentagon are rare compared to terrorist operations at the community level, which are meant to control local populations and are often targeted at women, gays, religious minorities or specific ethnic groups. As Gita Sahgal said in a 2007 speech for Amnesty International:

> Most acts of terrorism, in most parts of the world, are well sign posted by the groups that commit them. They are often carried out by people who know their targets well. Their aim is not only to murder and maim but to intimidate and control. In short, for civilians who are the targets of such attacks, the enemy is not unknown but an intimate one. And the threat of terrorism affects freedom of expression, freedom of movement, the right to education and to health and work as much as it threatens the right to life itself ...
>
> The Taliban puts up night letters warning teachers not to teach and children, especially girls, not to go to school. Recently they have issued warnings to barber shops to stop shaving men's beards. Islamist militants from Algeria to Iraq and Kashmir have threatened women who do not conform to the dress codes they impose or the curfews they enforce. Armed groups may intervene in disputes at community level, providing their own forms of summary justice. The IRA's practice of shooting offenders in the knee is an example. But such groups usually have a puritanical agenda as well.

Their purpose is not simply to attack the forces of the state or an occupying force but to impose control on the population that is supposed to be their support base.[180]

This is the politics of armed gangs who crave not liberation but dominance, whether they are narcotraficantes, self-styled revolutionaries, religious zealots, or all of the above. History has demonstrated that any political project – left or right – that relies on terror will not end by serving goals of liberation. A movement that tries to achieve power by blowing up ordinary citizens as they go to work or to market, or attend a wedding or a religious celebration, is not on the side of the people, and the people know it.

There are those who justify the notion that only equal violence can overtake the strength and violence of the ruling class, using the argument that, "One man's terrorist is another man's freedom fighter." But saying that the violence of one group is necessary to end the violence of another is like talking about "war to end war" – a World War I slogan. Violence breeds violence and the means shape the end. The feminist movement has stressed that the personal is political. Those who wish to transform society need to do so in ways that mobilize the positive transformational strengths of masses of people, rather than use methods of violence, dogmatism, and authoritarianism.

---

[180] Sahgal, G. "Negotiating Scylla and Charybdis – Human Rights and Terrorism". Speech at the AIUSA Public Roundtable. 16 February 2007. www.centreforsecularspace.org/?q=resources.

WRONG IDEA 5: ANY FEMINIST WHO CRITICIZES THE MUSLIM RIGHT IS AN ORIENTALIST AND ALLY OF US IMPERIALISM

At one point in her latest book, Leila Ahmed, the Harvard scholar of women and Islam, breaks into an anguished cry:

> I continue to believe ... that the rights and conditions of women in Muslim-majority societies often are acutely in need of improvement, as indeed they are in many other societies. But the question now is how we address such issues while not allowing our work and concerns to aid and abet imperialist projects, including war projects that mete out death and trauma to Muslim women under the guise and to the accompaniment of a rhetoric of saving them.[181]

It is a classic statement of the double bind, which has succeeded in making discussion of anything relating to Muslim women completely taboo in some circles and, in others, so hedged around by fearful qualifications as to be almost unintelligible.

Any feminist in the UK or North America who raises issues of gender politics in Muslim-majority countries is likely to be called an Orientalist; compared to Laura Bush, Ayan Hirsi Ali, and Irsad Manji; and accused of using "good Muslim-bad Muslim" stereotypes. If she is white, she will be told she is colonialist; if she is a woman of colour or feminist from the Global South, she will be considered to lack authenticity. She will be accused of "essentializing" political Islam and ignoring differences within it; of lacking nuance and failing to contextualize;

---

[181] Ahmed, op. cit., p. 229.

of having internalized ideas of Western superiority; of perpetuating binaries such as progressive vs. reactionary, liberal vs. conservative, secular vs. fundamentalist; of being a traitor to her community and culture. She will be beaten over the head with Edward Said, a self-described secularist who must be turning in his grave to see the use his followers make of him. Here, for example, is a recent discussion by Rupal Oza, director of the Women's and Gender Studies programme at Hunter College, and Amna Akbar, Senior Research Scholar and Advocacy Fellow at the Center for Human Rights and Global Justice and the International Human Rights Clinic of New York University Law School:

> [S]ecular feminists' concern that "Muslim fundamentalist" religious codes impose and sanction violence on women and queers relies on a myopia that understands Muslim women only as victims of Muslim men and Islam, ignoring the role of imperial violence in defining Muslim realities around the world … The military, intelligence, and humanitarian arms of the US "War on Terror" rely on the construction of Muslim men and Islam as savage threats, Muslim women as helpless victims and the United States as liberator-cum-saviour … The victim-savage-saviour framework produces one-dimensional narratives that marginalize or erase imperial violence and transnational and structural inequalities. In producing human rights subjects in clear-cut codependent categories of victim, savage, and saviour, these human rights discourses transform complex social contexts rife with inequalities and violence into neat moral geographies … this limited imagination of victims elides the ways in which imperial, secular violence – the US occupation of Afghanistan or US drone strikes in Yemen and Pakistan – undermine human rights

and material realities of men and women around the world.[182]

The message is clear: stick to US imperialism and shut up about the Muslim Right. While such a message is to be expected from the Muslim Right itself, this is coming from academic feminists and the message long predates 9/11. Academic postmodernism reached its zenith as part of the rightward political turn of the 1980s and 1990s, when globalized capital appeared triumphant and all hope of positive radical change faded; it is, in short, the politics of despair. Haideh Moghissi's critique of this tendency, *Feminism and Islamic Fundamentalism: The Limits of Postmodern Analysis*, was written two years before the attack on the World Trade Center. Says Moghissi:

> [M]y concern here is less with postmodernism as a slippery epistemological stance and more with its effect on our political climate and mood – its well-advertised but fictitious radicalism (which rapidly dissolves into a celebration of cultural difference), its privileging of the "local" (as against "master narratives" emphasizing universal rights) and, consequently, its curious affinity with the most reactionary ideas of Islamic fundamentalism. For the two share a common ground – an unremitting hostility to the social, cultural, and political processes of change and knowledge and rationality, originating in the West, known as modernity.[183]

---

[182] Akbar, A. and R. Oza. Forthcoming 2013. "'Muslim Fundamentalism' and Human Rights in the Age of Terror and Empire". M. Satterthwaite and J. Huckerby (eds.) *Gender, National Security and Counter-Terrorism: Human Rights Perspectives.* New York: Routledge.
[183] Moghissi, H. 1999. *Feminism and Islamic Fundamentalism.* London: Zed Books, p. 52.

The postmodernist feminist analysis has a curiously conservative view of Muslim women, with no room for the hundreds of millions of Muslim women who are secularist in the same way Christians, Hindus, and Jews are. Muslims are treated as people who must be protected from cosmopolitanism – this again echoes the view of the Muslim Right. As Sadia Abbas, assistant professor of English and Women's and Gender Studies at Rutgers University, points out, this kind of feminism ignores the actual views and organizations of women in Muslim-majority countries in order to defend the Muslim Right's construction of a beleaguered Islam facing off against the US empire:

> Does Islam really need that much help? Are arguments between Muslims simply irrelevant? Can coercive practices of subordinating women that seek Islamic authority ever be critiqued when they take place in contexts where Muslims face discrimination, and where there is the backdrop of a brutal and long colonial history? Are secular or reformist Muslim feminists allowed to talk about patriarchal structures that draw upon Islam or are they always to be subjected to disciplining by the metropolitan gaze... within the post-secularist universe there can be no secular or anti-Islamist Muslims or Muslim reformers. There is, in other words, a recurrent invocation of the plurality of Islamicate cultures and yet a continuous subsumption of most Muslims to the most orthodox kinds.[184]

Postcolonial postmodernist feminism seldom examines the political questions of alliance and affiliation taken up in this study, or the complicated dialectic between terrorism and counter-terrorism. The analysis has no room for the fact that the supposedly

---

[184] Abbas, S. "The Echo Chamber of Freedom: The Muslim Woman and the Pretext of Agency", *boundary 2*, forthcoming 2013.

"democratic" and "anti-imperialist" Muslim Brotherhood in Egypt is eager to get loans from the World Bank and accept US aid. Actually, the analysis has very little room for the real world at all – its focus is on image, representation and trope rather than relationships between living people. With the exception of wars of empire, real-world political battles fade away; there are no actual Islamist organizations, no political parties, no struggles over particular laws. In fact there are no social actors of any kind except for the US military and its drones, just "narratives", "categories" and "complex social constructs". Most of all, there is no way that progressives or feminists in the North can act in solidarity with those in the Global South, for any solidarity can only be construed as imperialist "rescue".

Yet solidarity is the only way to cut through the knots of the double bind.

A RADICAL SUGGESTION

Here is a radical suggestion for the Anglo-American left: Instead of allying with and protecting the Muslim Right, how about solidarity with actual popular movements of democrats and feminists struggling in the Global South? How about recognizing that we all face an emerging conservative front in which Washington and the Muslim Brotherhood are more likely to be allies than adversaries, and human rights are of no concern to either?

In a brief essay on economic and military history since the 1970s, Biju Mathew, an anti-Hindutva activist, public intellectual and organizer of the New York Taxi Workers Alliance, links the Muslim Right with neoconservative movements in the North and lays out an analysis of the political transformation necessary for the Anglo-American left:

> Even as the post-colonial dream of some basic equity soured across the Global South, we have seen the rapid rise of a range of neocon movements ... [that] have either influenced state power or directly controlled it over the last four decades (and driven imperial adventures), there has also been a rise of a distributed neoconservative trajectory across much of the Global South. The distributed and diverse Islamic neoconservative insurgencies represented by al-Qaeda or the Lashkar e Taiba, the al Shabaab or the Jaish e Mohammad are but the latest in that trend. In large part, I would argue, that the US left – both the white and people of color left – have failed to incorporate

these complexities into their analysis and action. The simplification of the field of left political action to a mere anti-imperialism instead of an anti-imperialism combined with solidarity has essentially worked to the advantage of the neoconservative movements across the world.[185]

In order to get its collective head straight, the Anglo-American left will have to overcome its imperial narcissism, in which the US (with its UK ally) is assumed to be the cause of everything bad happening in the world, and the only possible response to its overwhelming power and evil is a pained ironic stance, or, at best, a position of moral witness. Yes, the US invades other countries and sends drones to kill by night; nevertheless, like the UK before it, the US is an imperial power in decline, stretched beyond its means, with severe domestic problems. And while it continues to prop up old style military dictatorships in the Middle East and elsewhere in pursuit of oil, it is just as happy to ally with the Muslim Right in all its various forms – from political parties like the Muslim Brotherhood and Jamaat e Islami, to the Pakistani and Saudi governments, the Taliban and the dictators of Central Asia. Democracy, human rights, gender and gay rights may be invoked in State Department speeches but talk is cheap; what really matters is to keep the oil flowing and the financial markets from collapsing.

To carry out Mathew's suggestion of an "anti-imperialism combined with solidarity", we will have to start by seeing that there is convergence as well as opposition between the US and the Muslim Right, and supporting those in the Global South who fight domination by both. Afghanistan would be a good place to begin, particularly for feminists.

---

[185] Mathew, B. "Wrestling the Dinosaur: Reflections on the 9/11 Decade". *SAMAR (South Asian Magazine for Action and Reflection)*. 11 September 2011. http://samarmagazine.org/archive/articles/379.

Missteps by mainstream US feminists in the late 1990s, notably the troubled relationship between the Feminist Majority and the Revolutionary Association of the Women of Afghanistan (RAWA), laid political landmines on the grounds of feminist solidarity. More recently, while some women antiwar activists have been very vocal about drones and troop withdrawal, they have barely uttered a peep in support of the Afghan women's agenda – as if the fact that former First Lady Laura Bush said a few hypocritical words about Afghan women's human rights means that nobody else should ever mention them again. Lack of attention by Western feminists to the demands of Afghan women not only strengthens the Taliban; it supports the agenda of the US and its allies, which is to get out fast without dealing with the mess they made – a mess that can only be remedied by means of human rights, democracy, and reparative measures. The "victim-savage-saviour framework" denounced so indignantly by some academic feminists becomes a smokescreen for inaction, an excuse for failure to respond to repeated requests by Afghan civil society and women's organizations for solidarity and support. Solidarity is not "rescue" but recognition of mutual interdependence. Empowering Afghan women and civil society are preconditions for political stability, and such stability would make a difference to all of us by helping to prevent the next war, freeing up military money for domestic purposes and ensuring that Afghanistan is no longer a breeding ground for salafi-jihadi militants.

If solidarity with feminists and progressives in the South is essential for any hopeful political project in the North, so is defence of secular space. Since the end of the Cold War, secular spaces all over the world have come under siege by various forms of fundamentalism, and the instrumentalization of religion for political gain has become a problem in regions as varied as Eastern Europe, Central Asia, South Asia, Africa, South America, Western Europe and North America. In all these places, religious identity politics has muddied discussion of class, racism and discrimination against women and sexual minorities. Democratic governance is based on the idea that the authority of the state is delegated by the people rather than coming from God, and separation of the state from religion is essential to democracy because gender, religious minority and sexual rights are issues whenever human rights are limited by religion, culture, or political expediency.

A complete programme for social justice is beyond the scope of this study. But in order to cut through the double binds described above – so we can defend ourselves and others against terrorism and counter-terrorism, empower civil society, promote universal human rights and strengthen democracy – we must think about both solidarity and secularism. These are not the only social remedies needed in a world torn by conflict and poised on the brink of ecological disaster, but both are essential to our ability to move forward.

CENTRE FOR SECULAR SPACE

We have founded the Centre for Secular Space to address critical gaps in understanding of the relationship between terrorism, fundamentalism and peace and security, using a feminist analysis. We believe that strategic discussions of peace and security must expand to include secularism and universality, since one of the greatest sources of conflict in today's world is the mobilization of religion and culture for political gain.

Democratic governance is based on the idea that the authority of the state is delegated by the people rather than coming from God. Thus secularism – by which we mean the separation of the state from religion and of religion from the state – is essential to democracy. This separation is particularly important to women and to sexual, political and religious minorities, because gender, freedom of religion and sexual rights become issues whenever human rights are limited by religion, culture or political expediency.

The CSS has three goals: to strengthen secular voices, oppose and respond to religious fundamentalism of all kinds, and promote universality in human rights.

Under each of these goals we will do research and advocacy, create debates that can impact policy, and build research links between regions in the Global South and countries that are centres of migration.

AUTHOR

Meredith Tax is US Director of the Centre for Secular Space. She is a novelist, historian, and essayist and has been an activist in the US feminist movement since the late sixties. She blogs at http://www.meredithtax.org.

EDITORIAL GROUP

Ariane Brunet is Programme Director of the Centre for Secular Space. She was Coordinator of the Women's Rights Program at Rights and Democracy.

Anissa Hélie is a member of the Advisory Board of the Centre for Secular Space. She is former Executive Director of Women Living Under Muslim Laws.

Sara Hossain is a member of the Advisory Board of the Centre for Secular Space. She is a practicing human rights lawyer at the Supreme Court of Bangladesh.

Gita Sahgal is the Executive Director of the Centre for Secular Space. A writer and documentary filmmaker, she was inaugural Head of the Gender Unit at Amnesty International.